"We all know what it means to miss a divine appointment—that opportunity to touch someone with the good news about Jesus Christ—that is there for a moment and then gone. It's discouraging to miss these appointments, and after a while we give up and begin to ignore them. They come and go, unattended. This book will reawaken our awareness of these opportunities and will also give us the practical help we need to make the most of them."
>—Jim Petersen, missionary and author, *Church Without Walls*

"This is a valuable book on reaching lost people. It is birthed in real experience and deep passion that lost people need to be found. This book will help you be a better witness."
>—Dr. Bob Ricker, president, Baptist General Conference

"Paul said, 'Do the work of an evangelist and fulfill your ministry.' This much-needed book by those who are doing it will show you how to be an effective witness for Christ."
>—Dr. Neil T. Anderson, president emeritus,
>Freedom In Christ Ministries

"So many of today's Christians suffer from timidity in sharing their faith. They fear disappointment, rejection, or outright hostility. In their wonderful new book, *Divine Appointments*, Bob and Matthew Jacks give us clear, precise, and often amusing instruction in how to make God's Great Commission a daily reality in our lives."
>—Bill Bright, founder and chairman,
>Campus Crusade for Christ International

"*Divine Appointments* is a book written out of reality, not theory. Bob and Matthew Jacks have not only recorded real-life experiences in sharing the Good News of Christ, but also give incredible hope to the ordinary person to do the same. From the very first page, you will be drawn into their lives and encouraged in your own life. I have walked with them in their neighborhood and with their friends. This is the real thing."
>—Jerry White, Ph.D., president, The Navigators;
>author, *Making Peace with Reality*

# DIVINE APPOINTMENTS

*"Lord, open my eyes today
to a person who needs to know You,
and give me Your words to say."*

## BOB JACKS & MATTHEW R. JACKS
### WITH PAM MELLSKOG

INTERIOR ILLUSTRATIONS BY MATTHEW R. JACKS

## NAVPRESS

Bringing Truth to Life
P.O. Box 35001, Colorado Springs, Colorado 80935

## OUR GUARANTEE TO YOU

The Navigators is an international Christian organization. Our mission is to reach, disciple, and equip people to know Christ and to make Him known through successive generations. We envision multitudes of diverse people in the United States and every other nation who have a passionate love for Christ, live a lifestyle of sharing Christ's love, and multiply spiritual laborers among those without Christ.

NavPress is the publishing ministry of The Navigators. NavPress publications help believers learn biblical truth and apply what they learn to their lives and ministries. Our mission is to stimulate spiritual formation among our readers.

© 2002 by Bob Jacks and Matthew Jacks

ISBN 1-57683-290-2

Cover design by Dan Jamison
Cover photograph by Boden / Ledingham / Masterfile
Cover calligraphy background by Don Bishop / Artville
Interior illustrations by Matthew R. Jacks
Creative Team: Nanci McAlister, Greg Clouse, Amy Spencer, Pat Miller

Some of the anecdotal illustrations in this book are true to life and are included with the permission of the persons involved. All other illustrations are composites of real situations, and any resemblance to people living or dead is coincidental.

Unless otherwise identified, all Scripture quotations in this publication are taken from the HOLY BIBLE: NEW INTERNATIONAL VERSION® (NIV®). Copyright © 1973, 1978, 1984 by International Bible Society. Used by permission of Zondervan Publishing House. All rights reserved. Other versions used include the *New Revised Standard Version* (NRSV), copyright © 1989, by the Division of Christian Education of the National Council of the Churches of Christ in the USA, used by permission, all rights reserved; and the *King James Version* (KJV).

CIP DATA APPLIED FOR

Printed in the United States of America

1 2 3 4 5 6 7 8 9 10 / 06 05 04 03 02

*To Betty, my wife of forty-eight years and Matthew's mother. She is the one you will see woven into most of the stories in this book. It is her compassion and gift of mercy that inspired us to take gifts to Helen Propes, a single mother of two, on Christmas Eves in downtown Wilmington. It is her love for the brokenhearted that encouraged us to pick up Bill Jolly, a homeless man, each Sunday morning for church. These acts of kindness caused each of our three children to have a heart for those who go through private pain.*

*Without her model to follow, I am not sure I would have developed a heart for those outside the body of Christ. Her courage to keep divine appointments, whether with a Mafia drug runner or a hairdresser, has been a great inspiration to me.*

*Working in partnership with her has been one of the great joys of my life. My prayer is that God will give us many more years to partner in sharing His love with a broken world.*

—BOB

*Thanks to Pam Mellskog, who provided the* wow! *factor to our stories—and much, much more.*

—BOB AND MATTHEW

# CONTENTS

# CHAPTER ONE

# FOR "SUPER" CHRISTIANS ONLY?

### BY MATTHEW R. JACKS

*"Lord, I am delighted to obey Thee in this matter,"
and instantly the Son of God will press to the
front, and there will be manifested in my human
life that which glorifies Jesus.*

—OSWALD CHAMBERS, *MY UTMOST FOR HIS HIGHEST*, MAY 14

*We proclaim him, admonishing and teaching everyone with all wisdom, so that we may present everyone perfect in Christ. To this end I labor, struggling with all his energy, which so powerfully works in me.*

—COLOSSIANS 1:28-29

～　　～　　～

O N THAT RAINY MONDAY morning in October 1986, my mother answered the door to our 1788 Connecticut home expecting to meet a contract painter—not a Mafia man with a seven-inch stainless steel .44 Magnum in a hidden holster under his left arm and a Colt .38 Special tucked between his belt and the small of his back. Though she noticed his tattoos, scraggly long hair, bushy beard, and bleary brown eyes, she welcomed the burly man and his sidekick, Kenny, in with scarcely a second look. But she must have sensed something amiss— she did ask one question before they crossed the threshold: "Now, you boys don't drink on the job, do you?" she inquired in her high-pitched West Virginia accent.

"No, ma'am," the duo quickly mumbled in unison. They assured her that they did none of that on the clock.

"Well," she sighed while turning into the house, "that's an answer to prayer." She had moved twenty-two times since her wedding day and had fired plenty of painters along the way because they couldn't walk a straight line. Little did she know, these guys had been smoking pot on the way there. Furthermore, Bryan Marcoux's substance abuse had escalated to six joints daily and six-hundred-dollars worth of cocaine weekly—potentially lethal combinations for someone behind the wheel, much less for someone with a practiced trigger finger.

But that day, Bryan and his buddy arrived at our recently purchased house to paint the dark, low-slung halls on the second floor eggshell white—to do an honest day's work laundering some dirty money. That's all. They didn't plan on causing trouble.

As for my mother, Betty, her day seemed earmarked for nothing more than organizing the haphazardly stacked moving boxes and pulling newspaper off everything from antique crocks to the artwork of her children, now decades past their kindergarten days. She could anticipate only one bright spot on that gloomy day—a "divine appointment."

## Mysterious Matters

UNLIKE APPOINTMENTS made between dentist and patient, broker and investor, school principal and parents, divine appointments often involve completely unknown quantities. They are, by definition, mysterious and often surprising. The time, the place, the individuals involved—all the details rest in the Holy Spirit's PalmPilot, not ours.

For instance, my mother never suspected firepower beneath Bryan's clothing. And neither of my folks knew that they had unwittingly become his guinea pigs—that the Monday morning painting gig was his first in the business. By the same token, Bryan counted on making just one fresh start—not two. He had jotted down the 8 A.M. appointment and our address the week before. But what clue had he of my mother's lifelong zeal to meet wayfarers just like him? How could he guess the powerful Word she had hidden in her heart? Surely he never dreamed that our family considers anyone who sets foot on the property as heaven-sent—regardless of whether they arrive to dine, mow, wire, clean, plumb, build, peddle, or paint.

So, when Bryan first crossed our creaky wood floors, ladder in hand, my mother prayed for sensitivity and for guidance. This is her habit, her discipline of obedience, and her tap on God's grace. Was Bryan a divine appointment? Was there a reason beyond interior decorating for their meeting?

If she could have pulled up a background check on him, she may have gone shopping instead of sticking around. Though only twenty-four at the time, the green painter was a veteran drug runner for the New York City–based Bruno family (the notorious "mob") in his Waterbury, Connecticut, hometown. He had jumped into the world of organized crime as a teenager because it put him in the fast lane on wheels most young men can only lust after. Pocketing as much as five thousand dollars a day in drug transactions that took seconds, he eventually drove a hot-off-the-lot Corvette, a Fleetwood Cadillac, and a Harley Davidson. When on two wheels, he partied with the Hell's Angels and other biker gangs. Frankly, our only bridge to his world came from Hollywood, the newspaper, or pulp fiction.

"I had gold chains that would choke you, man," he glowers these days, squeezing his right hand and throwing a quick side-cut punch to audiences listening to his testimony. "I had my tattoo design taken down and carved into solid gold rings . . . and I'd had every relationship there was with all kinds of women."

But by 1986, this bad boy had also racked up some debt in the usual way, by spending more than he made. Despite a network of drug runners pushing beneath him in the Waterbury area, he got in hoc to the Mafia for a whopping sixty thousand dollars and to a New York motorcycle club for nineteen thousand before he ran for his life and showed up on our doorstep—jumpy with paranoia and heavily armed.

## REJOICING OVER LOST SOULS

WHILE TRUDGING past my mother that morning to lay canvas floor coverings upstairs, Bryan made a mental note of the Bible lying open on the table and of her comment about prayer. No one can number his or her days, but Bryan sensed a price on his head, and lately he had been obsessed with his mortality. So, after working a couple of hours with Kenny, he ambled downstairs to the kitchen for a break and inexplicably found himself making small talk with the petite woman sorting spoons and napkin rings.

"Tell me, Mrs. Jacks: If I die tomorrow, am I going to heaven or hell?" Bryan philosophically mused while sipping a cold glass of water and staring out the curtainless, paned window above the sink. All ears, she stopped fishing from the cardboard box and offered him a chair at our long, rough-hewn antique table. Sitting across from Bryan, she began to explain from her worn Bible that eternal security has more to do with a relationship than with a religion. They spent the next hour talking about sin before my mom, who had been down this road many times before, sensed it was time to ask him if he knew Christ in a personal way.

"Ma'am, I have *no* idea what you're talkin' about," he admitted slowly in his salty New England brogue.

Two hours later, he spied the clock. Time had flown while the paint dried upstairs. Worried about the "wasted" hours, he lurched his chair back to stand. My mom pointed out that their conversation was on her nickel, and she wasn't worried about the money. Then she cut to the chase.

"Bryan," she paused before asking her simple signature

question, "can you think of any reason you don't want to invite Christ into your life?"

The husky man looked away and grouched that she didn't know what kind of person he was. Our plaster walls, chock-full of two centuries' worth of stories, must have held their breath. The rain pounding outside may have misted a moment, waiting in the quietness that arced between the Bible study leader and the biker thug trying to cover his past with a paintbrush alone. Then she told him what Jesus wants all the world to hear—that the past doesn't matter, that His forgiveness comes without hindsight.

In Luke 15:7, Jesus said, "I tell you that in the same way there will be more rejoicing in heaven over one sinner who repents than over ninety-nine righteous persons who do not need to repent." My dad often paraphrases by saying heaven celebrates one lost soul coming to Christ in downtown Hartford's worst ghetto more than the ninety-nine bench warmers at a church business meeting in ritzy Simsbury.

However you picture it, the angels probably started somersaulting before Bryan broke the silence. He figured he'd find a prison cell or a casket before he found Christ. Everyone else did too. Yet, because my mom acted like Jesus with skin on, because she took the initiative to show him the redemption line and to invite him to cross it, she discovered that this bully had a teddy bear's heart.

Today, fifteen years later, Bryan still jokes that he surrendered his life and his will to Jesus Christ for seventy-five dollars (three hours at twenty-five an hour). But who can properly value the "vein of spiritual gold" struck in that single divine appointment—the one where Bryan switched places in the Holy Spirit's matchmaking book from unbeliever to believer?

Since then, he has married, fathered four children, and found his niche as a full-time associate pastor with a toll-free number for kids in crisis around the country. The bulk of his ministry success stems from frank confessions of both his wildly misspent youth and his total dependency on God's old-fashioned amazing grace. Miracles happen. And he often shares how he wasted seven years serving Satan as a racist drug runner before serving Christ on those same Waterbury streets as the Salvation Army's outreach coordinator.

For five years, he showed up on those streets day after day hoping for divine appointments with whites as well as blacks. And guess what? The Holy Spirit noted that availability and booked Bryan solid—from skid-row bums to bankers. With a new heart and a new hat, he even shared Christ with the chronically skittish drug traffickers he knew from his fast days in the business.

Today Bryan still sees countless people come to faith every year through his speaking engagements at youth rallies, in prisons, and one-to-one in restaurants, on street corners, or in airport terminals. He is now working with a ministry in Goldsboro, North Carolina, reaching the "captive and brokenhearted" primarily through his very successful street ministry.

My parents often say that if Bryan were the only convert-turned-disciple they had since moving to New England it would have been worth their relocation.

"If your life hasn't been radically changed," he challenges, "if you're the same way that you were last year as you are today, I don't believe that the Master's ever touched you. . . . If you read Scripture, everybody who *let* Jesus Christ touch them was radically changed."

## WHITE ELEPHANTS

BRYAN IS living proof. But not all divine appointments yield such a dramatic testimony and subsequent fruitfulness in God's kingdom. Still, my dad and I decided to write this book because we believe that at the heart of every authentic Christian conversion experience you'll find an intense private celebration. And we believe that God calls every Christian to make that celebration public—one person at a time.

By forwarding the notion of divine appointments, we hope to raise your awareness. If you have accepted Jesus Christ, you can trust that the Holy Spirit hovers in and around you at all times. And He's got big plans for each day that go beyond earning a living, caring for your family, and enjoying leisure time. The Holy Spirit appoints each of us to God's great welcoming committee. We all have a role in shaking hands with those for whom God is a stranger and in sharing His love through word and deed. But without this awareness—without deliberately being "on call" for Spirit-inspired meetings—we may completely overlook countless opportunities.

While raising awareness flattens one of the biggest obstacles between you and the next possibility, fear remains. That explains why those aware of divine appointments may choose not to keep them. My dad knows a man who rose in the ranks of the Connecticut State Police and eventually delved into the murky world of forensic science. Throughout his career, Major Timothy Palmbach has chased dangerous suspects and picked through crime scenes of murder, arson, rape, and theft. He accepted Christ nearly thirty years ago but admits that nothing makes him more nervous than the thought of sharing his faith in Christ.

Many other well-meaning, authentic Christians balk when they sense the Holy Spirit arranging encounters with unbelievers. It's like someone yanks the pin and, *whoosh,* the white elephant of fear instantly inflates. This fear puffs up and invisibly crowds the room, pressing the believer and the unbeliever apart. In this way, fear—not faith— becomes the focus.

We may all feel a little anxious about keeping divine

appointments because of the potential rejection, disappointment, discouragement, and even embarrassment. Beyond the obvious, though, there's also the plain fear of going it alone.

As a kid, I assumed that all Christian families trusted the Holy Spirit to be tirelessly putting believers in contact with unbelieving friends, relatives, colleagues, acquaintances, and strangers. I grew up thinking this was a norm in the Christian community. Now, as a thirty-eight-year-old, I appreciate that my family's view of the Holy Spirit's presence and power in these appointments may be somewhat novel. Why? I have a hunch that it's because the Holy Spirit remains the most anonymous member of the Trinity, a fuzzy face and unfamiliar voice even to those who call Jesus Christ Lord.

Part of the image problem stems from His characteristic behind-the-scenes activity. Like a director working during a live performance, He can only whisper from the wings to actors fighting stage fright. However, those who listen to that voice coming from around the cranberry-colored velvet curtains will hear stage directions that call for crossing paths with unbelievers in one scene or another.

On the stage of life, we call these crossings "divine appointments." Yet the Holy Spirit never forces these intersections or holds actors to a scripted dialogue—a verbatim reading. Rather, He gently coaches while continually scouting the audience for fresh talent. If He spots an individual who will leave the anonymity of his or her seat, take to the stage, and remain open to direction—well, more divine appointments are in the making.

## A Myth Debunked

SINCE 1965, when I was still in diapers, my mom and dad have both been ready and willing to share their faith whenever opportunities appear. They've by now met and ministered to a whole eclectic village of people scattered near and far—from ex-Mafia men like Bryan to doctors and lawyers, from the bereaved slumped on hospital lounge couches to hairdressers and self-made multimillionaires. Some may think my folks are "super" Christians—that their success in sowing so many seeds of faith and reaping so many souls for Christ stems from special God-given gifts. If you knew them, you might think the same.

It's true that my mother has the gift of mercy, my father has the gift of teaching, and both of them have an extraordinary gift of evangelism. So for a long time, I figured that the Holy Spirit scheduled divine appointments mostly with "gifted" people like Betty and Bob Jacks. They seem to have the right stuff. Furthermore, unlike Bryan and me, they don't have the other stuff—a history of life going haywire. Their track record shows none of the red-tagged issues like promiscuity or substance abuse that make practicing the Christian lifestyle—much less sharing Christ—seem ludicrous. Why would the Holy Spirit count on me for a divine appointment when people like my parents are handy?

Unfortunately, the "For Super Christians Only" mindset sabotages countless possibility-laden exchanges every day—just like fear and the lack of awareness. I never felt like a super Christian, so I checked out in my early twenties. I wasn't totally anti-God or anti-church. I just stopped practicing my faith and started ignoring opportunities to share it. Like a professor on sabbatical, I stayed loosely connected with the institution without ever showing up on campus to pick up my mail, return phone calls, or chance meeting with others who might ask about my time off.

After graduating from Philadelphia's University of the Arts in 1986—the same year my mother led Bryan to Christ in our kitchen—I resolutely closed the Bible and tossed my appointment book with God. I split with my previous life of affluent suburban living and evangelical faith and began running from place to place in search of a new identity—from Santa Fe to Staten Island to Chicago to Manhattan and back and forth from Connecticut to Maine. I eventually settled in Philadelphia to rehab an inner-city brownstone as a bona fide Bohemian.

One summer afternoon, while sitting on my South Philly stoop talking on the phone, I saw a pack of ten young men shoot one of their peers about twenty times by the fire hydrant at the end of my block. The cheapness of life in the throes of that drug dispute seared one of the most surreal memories into my brain. In that frenzied moment, with chatter continuing through the receiver still pressed hard against my ear, I remember thinking with alarming Doonesbury-like detachment, *He's dead already. You don't have to keep shooting him.*

But at the time, it didn't seem to matter how my lifestyle skewed my good judgment and tempted me further from faith. On the surface, I was making it without fully committing to God. I enjoyed the darker side of the artist's urban underworld with its smoky counterculture. In the early 1990s, I had friends, I had fun, and I had landed a coveted job as assistant exhibit director at the fourth largest museum in the nation—the Philadelphia Museum of Art. However, when Philly's crime rate spiked to an historic high, I escaped to Lancaster, Pennsylvania, to live with a jazz singer while I made folk art and antique furniture reproductions full-time among the Amish.

I expected my live-in to sing in piano bars most nights, but I didn't anticipate finding her unfaithful. When she left me in February 1996, I curled into a tight ball on the double bed that seemed like a sprawling island in the cramped farmhouse I was rehabbing.

Soon, the disarray, pressing silence, solitude, and cold

confronted all my stumblings in every imaginable area. I wasn't suicidal, but I felt horrible about my entire life. So I begged God to forgive me, to give me another chance to make something of me. And instantly, I kid you not, I had this smile on my face when I realized I had been forgiven for ten years of rebellion. What's more, I debunked the myth of super Christians. When I finally rejected *it*—not God—I was able to make that total commitment to Him.

## YOUR STATION

LOOKING BACK, I realize how completely parting company with other Christians left me more vulnerable to temptation. I feel like I squelched my spiritual growth and squandered so many divine appointments while wandering. And I regret grieving my family—all of whom kept me in prayer throughout. Yet I also consider those days and nights in Philly that stretched into years as a valuable immersion experience with lost people.

This crowd seemed disinterested at best and hostile at worst toward the gospel. But that perception props up another barrier to keeping divine appointments. This mindset puts me (rather than the Holy Spirit) in charge of picking the people who seem ready to receive Christ. In reality, you just never know whom He'll bring along to your station in life.

In this sense, the divine appointments concept reminds me of the road-atlas-sized scheduling book at my mom's beauty salon, a place where she has led all but one of her hairstylists to Christ in the past thirty-five years. At quitting time, the salon's smudged book with the Olympic rings of coffee stains reflects the day's activity. Checks mark one of three columns behind each penciled-in name—showed, rescheduled, and canceled.

Clients who keep their appointments demonstrate that they are serious about a positive change. Some even arrive holding a magazine clipping of the kind of cut and style they want. Others reschedule because they have neither the time nor the energy to think about changing now, but still hope to do so in the future. Those who cancel have accepted what they look like, at least for the time being. They have no pressing need for change. If the receptionist tallied each of the three columns daily and then crunched a year's worth of those numbers, she could accurately predict the percentage rate at which the salon's clients showed, rescheduled, or canceled.

Every day, the receptionist expects to scratch some names. In contrast, she counts on the salon staff to show up at their stations for each appointment she books. She trusts them to be prepared to shampoo, condition, cut, perm, and style all kinds of hair—blond to black, straight to curly, brittle to silken. However, without staff faithfully posted, she faces a labor crunch that may force her to turn people away at the door. And being short-staffed, there's of course no way she can accommodate walk-ins.

## Near Misses

MOST AUTHENTIC Christians acknowledge the Great Commission Christ gave in Matthew 28:18-20:

> "All authority in heaven and on earth has been given to me. Go therefore and make disciples of all nations, baptizing them in the name of the Father and of the Son and of the Holy Spirit, and teaching them to obey everything that I have commanded you. And remember, I am with you always, to the end of the age" (NRSV).

We know that Jesus calls us to share our faith with unbelievers, but how many times has it seemed like the barriers discussed in this chapter just won't budge? Take heart. Even so-called "professional" Christians wrestle to keep appointments and to believe that a blessing's afoot.

Sometimes divine appointments lead to sharing your testimony or the Four Spiritual Laws. Other times, they may involve simply showing kindness, generosity, pardon, or friendship. Your willingness to meet the unbeliever with God's love in mind may produce thankfulness or thanklessness, but you'll never know until you show.

# KEEPING
## APPOINTMENTS

1. The Jacks family prays for divine appointments with anyone who steps on their property. Would you consider adopting the same mindset? Why or why not?

2. Why do you suppose Bob left Betty alone to greet two strangers that morning?

3. Do you think that sharing the gospel with a member of the opposite sex is appropriate? If so, what precautions could you take in these situations?

4. Do you think Betty would have had the same boldness to share with Bryan had she known of his involvement with the underworld? Why or why not?

5. Matthew Jacks grew up trusting the Holy Spirit to put believers in contact with unbelievers. Is that your expectation? Why or why not? If not, how could your church or parachurch group encourage this belief?

# CHAPTER TWO

# 24/7 AVAILABILITY

### BY BOB JACKS

*Are you prepared to abandon entirely and let go?*
*. . . Abandonment means to refuse yourself the*
*luxury of asking questions.*

—OSWALD CHAMBERS, *MY UTMOST FOR HIS HIGHEST*, APRIL 28

*When they had finished eating, Jesus said to Simon Peter, "Simon son of John, do you truly love me more than these?"*

*"Yes, Lord," he said, "you know that I love you."*

*Jesus said, "Feed my lambs."*

—JOHN 21:15

❧　❧　❧

"THIS IS IT," I sighed as a bittersweet feeling of victory washed over me. "Dallas Theological Seminary, here I come." I stacked my beat-up leather Bible, notes, and Bill Bright's dog-eared workbook *The Christian and the Holy Spirit,* and flopped back into an overstuffed floral lawn chair on our sun porch in utter resignation.

Three years of soul searching and resistance brought me to that July day in 1966 when, at age thirty-four, I finally decided to let Christ take total control of my life. Reclining in my early-morning solitude, I admired the dawn gradually warming the black night sky into lavender, magenta, and marigold. And I silently fretted about my dim future. I figured it held a passport to Zimbabwe, if not seminary enrollment. Frankly, both options looked like buckets of ice-cold water tipped to douse the hot research-engineering career I had toiled long and hard to wire at DuPont. The only people I knew who were having real impact on a lost world were either pastors or full-time parachurch staff workers.

What's more, I felt that familiar pressure to be perfect increasing, which also made me squirm. Mere carnal temptations seemed beneath the "totally committed" believers I knew, those precious few full-timers who looked like they lived absolutely above reproach. I considered them the crème de la crème of the Christian faith—an ultra-righteous vanguard marching before us stragglers who couldn't manage to hold rank, much less goose step.

It was as if a cosmic cookie cutter stamped a generic lifestyle on folks filled with and controlled by the Holy Spirit. So I imagined that my transformation would plant me in a culture akin to that of a strict order of monks with vows of poverty, penitence, and chastity required.

Why *wouldn't* God take advantage of a believer's new-found availability in order to cover the more extreme areas of service? Surely He needed willing souls to fill empty seats in some "key" vocations—from studying in ivory-towered seminaries and exhorting behind ornate oak pulpits to serving on hardscrabble foreign mission fields where safe drinking water and a common language could prove scarce. Despite such fears, that morning I surrendered every ounce of my will and prepared to hit the books or the road for Jesus, ASAP.

## PIE TO PASTA

I SCRATCH my head these days and wonder how such powerful misperceptions mushroom throughout the Christian subculture, because it turns out my concerns weren't grounded in truth. I soon learned that the call of the totally committed Christian need not be narrowly defined as full-time ministry vocations or encased in a shiny plastic shell of "do's and don'ts" perfectionism. Yet how many believers shy away from giving God sole control, based on those stereotypes?

Granted, when I made myself 100 percent available to do Christ's bidding—not mine—I correctly anticipated that

He could pull all my props, all those people and things that gave me a sense of purpose, security, and happiness. Letting Him control my treasures and toys seemed as perilous as hang gliding off the south rim of the Grand Canyon minus lessons, or skiing a black diamond slope without poles.

Yet I surrendered on the sun porch because deep down I knew that I had missed my fullest blessing and my fullest opportunity to be a blessing. I had accepted Christ at age sixteen, married a Christian woman, and served God at a handful of Bible-based churches as a deacon, elder, Sunday school teacher, usher, and committee member. I showed up for services on Sunday mornings and Wednesday nights, but was I available for divine appointments 24/7?

Not a chance. I compartmentalized my belief in Christ as if it were a clean-cut slice of apple pie. Faith fit snugly in the round tin next to the other slices of life—family, career, leisure, education, plans, thoughts, possessions. But after so many years of living in this orderly, pre-dictable way, I started feeling spiritually half-baked. I scrapped the pie for a bowl of spaghetti and let the Lord integrate like olive oil throughout—to where I couldn't separate one part of my life from another.

## DRIVER VERSUS PASSENGER

ULTIMATELY, I concluded that the drama of Christian living often unfolds in two distinct acts of faith: accepting Christ as Savior and later committing all to Him. In the first act, you invite God into your life. In the second, after you've had more time to know Him, you trust Him to control your life.

This difference reminds me of when we celebrated our firstborn son Michael's fifteenth birthday. At that magic age, our then home state of Delaware considered him competent to practice driving. I thought that would be great, as long as he could drive the school's vehicles—not ours! Nevertheless, I complied with the driver's education course requirements. I approved of him getting a learner's permit and agreed to accompany him as he logged practice hours behind the wheel.

As we drove together, I felt reasonably comfortable giving him the wheel in areas I considered safe. I felt okay letting him tootle around the neighborhood on memorized routes to and from church, school, and the grocery store. But letting him take off to Wilmington on the freeway seemed nuts, in no way wise. I preferred to snatch the wheel and switch seats, thereby reestablishing the way we had driven in the past as father and son, driver and passenger.

Many believers love Christ and accept Him as Savior. They will buckle up and let God drive them to church and around their suburb. But boy, letting Him be in control out there in the real world—with its heavy traffic, high speeds, competition, mergers, and road rage—that's a whole other story. When the rubber hits the road, they grab the wheel, and Jesus is back to just being along for the ride. But without Him at the wheel, you will sooner or later crash.

## White Funerals

OSWALD CHAMBERS, author of the classic devotional *My Utmost For His Highest*—a best-seller since 1935—calls this second critical leap of faith a "white funeral." It marks your last day as a rebel fighting God's will, the day when He hears you finally say, "Thy will be done. Here are the keys, Lord Jesus." You will then scoop the final shovelfuls of dirt on your old life to focus fully on your new life in Christ, your Christ-controlled life.

Sounds grim, but this concept rings true with a central New Testament teaching. In Galatians 2:20, Paul stated, "I have been crucified with Christ and I no longer live, but Christ lives in me." Therein lies the importance of the white funeral. Without burying your old life, the Holy Spirit cannot completely move in and take charge.

Not surprisingly, Chambers understood this: white funerals make space for divine appointments. In a journal entry entitled "Circumstances," he wrote:

> The circumstances of a saint's life are ordained of God. In the life of a saint, there is no such thing as chance. God by His providence brings you into the circumstances that you cannot understand at all, but the Spirit of God understands. God is bringing you into places and among people and into conditions in order that the intercession of the Spirit in you may take a particular line.
>
> Never put your hand in front of the circumstances and say, "I am going to be my own providence here, I must watch this and guard that." All your circumstances are in the hand of God. Therefore, never think it strange concerning the circumstances you are in. Your part in the intercessory prayer is not to enter into the agony of intercession, but to utilize the common-sense circumstances God puts you in and the common-sense people He puts you amongst by His providence, to bring them before God's throne and give the Spirit in you a chance to intercede for them. In this way, God is going to sweep the whole world with His saints. . . .
>
> Your intercessions can never be mine, and my intercessions can never be yours, but the Holy Ghost makes intercession in our particular lives without which intercession someone will be impoverished.[1]

Chambers encouraged laity to partake just as fully in divine appointments as clergy, and he led by example. Regardless of the time, place, and individuals involved, he modeled 24/7 availability and penned this conviction: "I am not appealed to on the line that I am of more use in certain places. *It is with me where He wills.* Bless the Lord, He guides. Pay attention to the source, and He will look after the outflow."[2]

Chambers' life reflects "outflow" that mine never will. From 1906 to 1910, he ran an itinerant Bible-teaching ministry in the United States, the United Kingdom, and Japan. Soon after, in 1911, he founded the Bible Training College in Clapham, London, and served as president and lecturer there until it closed in 1915 because of World War I. He then sailed for Egypt (near Cairo), where he ministered to Australian and New Zealand troops as a YMCA chaplain before dying in 1917 after surgery for a ruptured appendix.

## THE BUILDING BLOCKS

YET I'M convinced few people will give God this kind of résumé when they reach the pearly gates, because few people are called to this type of work. Instead of stepping into the role of a "professional" Christian who serves in formal full-time ways, most will instead contribute informally as "plainclothes" believers.

For the plainclothes believer, offering God 24/7 availability involves three key building blocks: seeing the locals with fresh eyes, trusting Him to use your time and resources wisely, and remaining transparent. Start by taking a second look at the people who populate familiar landscapes—your neighborhood, workplace, local post office, day-care facility, dry cleaner, or favorite restaurant. From this perspective, divine appointments will crop up as you go about your daily business. Who knows what spiritual fruit could come from interchanges with the supermarket clerk scanning your cornflakes or the neighbor out walking Fido or the coworker tapping the water cooler?

Plainclothes believers, no matter how Type A, also do well to trust Him with their time. Jesus didn't waste His time on "accidental" contacts, and if He is living His life through you, He won't waste your time either. Besides, your time is now His time, because you gave Him your clock and a blank sheet of paper, and you surrendered your right to punch out. He uses divine appointments for His purposes, whether you can perceive them or not. Those purposes may include a warm apple pie for a new neighbor.

Finally, plainclothes believers must remain transparent in every area of daily life—from marketplace interactions to the relationships developing under their own roof. Let those who know you see Christ in you, warts and all.

## CAREER HAT CHANGE

MY CAREER hat changed drastically about ten years after I made this "no holds barred" commitment. A close cousin of mine, Ted Crew, who was working for a large oil company, called and asked me if I would consider becoming his partner in an interstate truck stop. Problem was, I was already counting on getting a retirement check from DuPont. The perks from working with such a great company could hardly be measured. A forty-hour-a-week job in a high-tech Engineering Research and Development department to a truck stop? About the only thing I knew that would help in this new endeavor was how to make homemade vegetable soup.

After much prayer by Betty, the kids, and me, I left DuPont and became an owner-operator of the largest truck stop in New England. I vividly recall Betty saying at a going-away dinner at our church, "Consider us your missionaries to New England." Shortly after arriving there, we recognized we were in one of the greatest mission fields in the world. We started doing evangelistic home Bible studies, out of which came our book, *Your Home a Lighthouse,* and a ministry by the same name.

## A PLAINCLOTHES MODEL

MY GRANDMOTHER Crew was as plainclothes a believer as they come—illiterate and poor. While I never sat in a pew or looked through stained glass as I was growing up in Parkersburg, West Virginia, her softly spoken evening prayers awakened my first God-consciousness. Now I know that it was her faith-filled voice that helped ready my heart to receive Christ as a teenager at a local church's youth event.

She lived in a four-room shanty with a rusty tin roof on Weed Knob, a high spot in the Appalachian boondocks with great vistas of three other counties in the distance. Two lethargic cows, a dozen clucking chickens, and a small herd of wobbly-kneed lambs puttered around her farm—a remote place with no plumbing or electricity during her lifetime. But these hardships didn't faze me as a kid.

I considered her place holy ground. Though Spartan, the one bedroom on the second floor felt like a cozy dorm room. Up there, I slept on a feather tick mattress in a squeaky bed next to hers and enjoyed our evening ritual. She would tuck me in, blow out the kerosene lamp on the small nightstand, and then pray aloud in the inky darkness.

My grandmother wore her long gray hair in a tight bun. Every morning, she put on an apron made from feed sacks and broke a sweat on her patch of acreage. She seemed made of iron, but her tender evening prayers always stuck with me long after my visit ended. As far as I know, she didn't consider herself an anointed prayer warrior—someone especially gifted at bending God's ear or, for that matter, the ears of her squirrelly, unchurched grandson. But she had faith, and she let it shine.

## ORDINARY JOE JESUS

JESUS, THE author of divine appointments, appeared to be a plainclothes player rather than a high priest. The second half of Isaiah 53:2 reads, "He had no beauty or majesty to attract us to him, nothing in his appearance that we should desire him." However, Hollywood forgets he was a carpenter and drapes a gathered off-white robe on Him. As a result, He loses so much of His plainclothes appeal in the twenty-first century. I realize that the director dresses Him that way in keeping with the spirit of historical accuracy. Yet, to modern eyes, He looks a little gussied up—even a little angelic without the visible halo and wings.

If I were in charge of those productions, I'd close the distance between then and now by revamping His getup to something more contemporary. He needs the garb of a carpenter, which brings Him into real time, threads that more accurately convey His disarming informality. So I would ship the robe to the Smithsonian as a replica and dress Him in duds that wouldn't easily get caught in a saw's teeth or noticeably soiled next to a toolbox. Faded Levis, a T-shirt, a worn Interstate Battery baseball cap, and scuffed steel-toed boots fit the bill. The facial hair and ponytail could stay in the picture because it resembles what many carpenters look like today.

Seriously, though, during his three years of public ministry, Jesus passed as an ordinary Joe, and He led a band of mostly blue-collar men who shared the same low profile. Of this motley crew, I think Peter makes the best example of a plainclothes believer. Reeking like fish, with dirt under his fingernails, and plodding with clay feet, he hardly seems the noble stuff of sainthood as captured in statues and oil paintings. Perfection seemed so far past Peter's reach. This man distinguished himself as the first to deny Jesus.

On the other hand, despite echoes of the crowing rooster, Peter was also the first to repent, and the one Christ counted on to keep a biggie-sized divine appointment—Pentecost—where three thousand believed in Jesus as Messiah. His ministry, like mine, took off after a defining moment—when He gave Jesus total control of his life and circumstances. Not surprisingly, the action took place far from the temple as the resurrected Jesus cooked on the beach at dawn.

## DEFINING MOMENTS

REFLECTING ON that tender scene in John 21 of Jesus waiting with breakfast reminds me of the time I fished in the Chesapeake Bay. After fishing offshore when it was pitch-black, I watched the morning break and the fog clear. I imagine Peter viewed a similarly hazy transition from night to light with the same serenity I enjoyed—until he spotted a ghostly silhouette at the water's edge.

"Catch any fish, boys?" Jesus shouted from the shore. When Peter identified Jesus only a hundred yards away, he splashed into the water and paddled to greet Him well before the boat's hull slid into the sand. Of course, Peter had phenomenal business to report. After dropping their nets to the other side as Jesus had suggested earlier, they snapped more than a few lines hauling 153 fish aboard.

As they celebrated and feasted on fresh fish and bread over the ring of hot coals, Jesus began dealing more deeply with Peter. He prodded him for a total commitment by asking, "Do you truly love me more than these?" If by "these" Jesus had meant the breakfasting boat fellows, wouldn't He have said "them"? Instead, He said "these." So perhaps He had gestured toward the beached boat, the well-used equipment, and the still-squirming pile of fish. Though this inquiry stung, perhaps it caused Peter to take stock—to rank the tools of his trade and the perks of his lifestyle next to the man he called Master.

"Hmmm," Peter may have mused. "One hundred and fifty-three fish multiplied by twenty bucks a fish equals 3,060 dollars. And the boat and the nets are worth at least . . . " Besides the business, Jesus wanted Peter to weigh his comfort zone too—the smell of the open sea, the culture of the coastal villages, his family and friends, the lifestyle of a harmless marauder.

Instead of surrendering, Peter stalled: "Lord, what about him?" he asked regarding another disciple standing nearby. Reading between the lines, I have a hunch that what Peter really wanted to know was, "Jesus, if I make a total commitment to you, where will I be going, and what will I be doing there?" To deepen the mystery, Jesus then implied that the other man might miraculously live until He returned. Peter's defining moment dawned when he realized that God only issues individual designer plans— even to people who dress down.

History tells us that Peter made the right decision. History doesn't tell us what happened to the boats and nets. That's a detail. God is in the detail business.

## BECOMING A GLOVE FOR GOD

DOES KEEPING divine appointments still seem like some-one else's opportunity? Perhaps you have resisted giving

God total control for all the standard-issue reasons—for the potential risk of leaving hearth and homeland, stepping off the career ladder, or simply living day to day following someone else's priority list. In *The Christian and the Holy Spirit,* Campus Crusade founder Bill Bright lists some other reasons that may cause you to hang an "Out to Lunch" sign indefinitely. Which of these availability squelchers apply to you?

- An exalted feeling of your own importance
- Love of human praise
- Anger and impatience
- Self-will, stubbornness, unteachability
- A compromising spirit
- A jealous disposition
- Lustful, unholy actions
- Dishonesty
- Unbelief
- Selfishness
- An unnatural love of money, beautiful clothes, cars, houses, or land[3]

I could spill some ink checking the ones that applied to me. Yet, when I surrendered my will to God, they vanished. From time to time, I pick up one or two. But during those battles, I cling to the fact that the war is over. Indeed, Colossians 2:9-10 reads, "In Christ all the fullness of the Deity lives in bodily form, and you have been given fullness in Christ, who is the head over every power and authority."

If you still feel like a bottom-of-the-barrel candidate for heaven-sent opportunities, remember that it's God's power—not yours—that keeps your head up and your knees from buckling. Paul reminds us in Philippians 2:13, "It is God who works in you to will and to act according to his good purpose." We have the victory. All we have to do is claim it.

For this reason, giving God 24/7 availability reminds me of trying on gloves. Companies manufacture them in many shapes, sizes, and materials—wool, leather, latex, and so on—for many purposes. Pairs of them lifelessly hang off hooks or lie in bins. But with strong hands inside, they can yank weeds from a flower garden, brush snow off a windshield, change a tire, or pull a tooth.

At the point of total commitment, you let Jesus Christ control you as a hand controls a glove. His hands provide the appropriate skill, stamina, sensitivity, and power needed to reach out to others. Acts 1:8 records Jesus promising as much to His disciples and to us: "But you will receive power when the Holy Spirit comes on you; and you will be my witnesses in Jerusalem, and in all Judea and Samaria, and to the ends of the earth."

Believers without this type of filling are like dry sponges. Until they let the Holy Spirit saturate them with Jesus' living water, they must be hard-pressed before they can share much more that a drop—if that. On the other hand, for those saturated, the slightest nudge or squeeze is enough pressure to produce a cup of this living water for someone else to taste. It's just as Jesus promised the woman at the well in John 4.

## THE HOLY SPIRIT'S HATS

PETER HAD *literally* walked with Christ for three years, but until that early-morning conversation—that defining moment with the Lord—he was still holding an independence flag. If your flag's still flying, remember that Jesus seeks a preponderance of plainclothes people, all of whom fall short of perfection. If you could be a peak performer at all times, you wouldn't need the Holy Spirit's indwelling.

Face facts. Living a Spirit-filled life of faith means that you may frequently not have the foggiest idea of what's next. Why? Because *you're not in charge anymore.* Where you go, what you do, and whom you meet pose constant question marks to a totally committed believer.

Sure, you may have visions of doing this or that, but uncertainty marks the footsteps of one following Jesus Christ. This kind of faith puts you in a perpetual free-float! However, when you invite Christ to take control 24/7, He wears a collection of hats and you can live confident of one thing—His competence and care, whatever the details. Don't sweat the details. In these roles, He brings:

∾ *the Spirit of God.* "Don't you know that you yourselves are God's temple and that God's Spirit lives in you?" (1 Corinthians 3:16).

∾ *the Spirit of Christ.* "You, however, are controlled not by the sinful nature but by the Spirit, if the Spirit of God lives in you. And if anyone does not have the Spirit of Christ, he does not belong to Christ" (Romans 8:9).

∾ *the Spirit of life.* "Through Christ Jesus the law of the Spirit of life set me free from the law of sin and death" (Romans 8:2).

∾ *the Spirit of truth.* "But when he, the Spirit of truth, comes, he will guide you into all truth. He will not speak on his own; he will speak only what he hears, and he will tell you what is yet to come" (John 16:13).

∾ *the Spirit of grace.* "How much more severely do you think a man deserves to be punished who has trampled the Son of God under foot, who has treated as an unholy thing the blood of the covenant that sanctified him, and who has insulted the Spirit of grace?" (Hebrews 10:29).

∾ *the Spirit of promise.* "And you also were included in Christ when you heard the word of truth, the gospel of your salvation. Having believed, you were marked in him with a seal, the promised Holy Spirit, who is a deposit guaranteeing our inheritance until the redemption of those who are God's possession—to the praise of his glory" (Ephesians 1:13-14).

# KEEPING
## APPOINTMENTS

1. Can you recall exactly when you accepted Christ? If so, did you give Him total control of your life then?

2. What keeps a believer from giving up everything?

3. Oswald Chambers calls the total commitment experience a "white funeral." What does this mean to you?

4. Bob Jacks calls his grandmother a plainclothes Christian. What does that mean?

5. How can Jesus Christ operate through you to reach those in your world today?

6. What do you need to do to be available as a plainclothes Christian?

7. Which availability squelcher most holds you back?

8. Can you be honest with the Lord and give Him that thing—or just confess you are going to hold onto it?

# CHAPTER THREE

# THE REST OF THE STORY

### BY MATTHEW R. JACKS

*If we are devoted to the cause of humanity, we shall soon be crushed and broken-hearted for we shall often meet with more ingratitude from men than we would from a dog; but if our motive is to love God, no ingratitude can hinder us from serving fellow men.*

—OSWALD CHAMBERS, *MY UTMOST FOR HIS HIGHEST*, FEBRUARY 23

*[Jesus said,] "But whoever drinks the water I give him will never thirst. Indeed, the water I give him will become in him a spring of water welling up to eternal life."*

*The woman said to him, "Sir, give me this water so that I won't get thirsty and have to keep coming here to draw water."*

—John 4:14-15

$\sim$     $\sim$     $\sim$

WHEN THE TRAIN CONDUCTOR spotted a blue-and-white 1950s sedan stalled on the tracks in Abilene, Texas, he snapped to attention and frantically blasted his horn five times. Seconds later, he sickened to see a full carload of passengers still grappling inside to escape. Jamming on the breaks proved futile. The long chain of wheels simply froze and screeched on the hot steel rails and unavoidably led to horror that December 29, 1961.

Behind the picture windows of a nearby café, an afternoon coffee klatch stopped mid-sip to peer wide-eyed at the dazzling sparks rooster-tailing over billows of coal-black engine smoke. Then the pug nose of the train savagely rammed the forlorn car, crushing it like an empty soda can before sloughing it off like a loose leaf of yesterday's newspaper.

When the paramedics arrived on the scene, they believed their hunt for life was over before it began. Who could survive in a car so mangled?

Rescue workers call the first hour after such accidents "golden" because it's the most priceless time to treat trauma, often the only time to treat it successfully. In this case, the lives at stake included Mrs. Alfano, her three daughters—identical five-year-old twins Rosalinda and LaDonna as well as their toddler sister, Patricia—and Mrs. Alfano's neighbor and two sons. The women had piled the children into the car to run an errand to the grocery store when their vehicle spluttered and inexplicably stalled in harm's way.

## SURVIVORS

THE NEIGHBOR and one of her sons survived, as did LaDonna. She dodged death when the train's tremendous impact snapped open the car's right rear door and popped her out like a champagne cork. In the meantime, her sister Patricia died instantly, while her mother and twin sister kept only a slippery grip on life.

Paramedics rushed to triage Mrs. Alfano and Rosalinda first because they seemed like the most likely hangers-on. LaDonna, on the other hand, looked as good as dead. Being thrown from the car had split open her face, exposing muscle, bone, and part of her brain. However, given her stubbornly persistent heartbeat, paramedics took her to the local hospital where a helicopter whisked her to San Antonio to be examined by a neurosurgeon. Though pessimistic about her chances, he inserted a steel brace to hold the hemispheres of her head together.

Rosalinda died on New Year's Eve; Mrs. Alfano passed away twenty-four hours later on New Year's Day. Only LaDonna pulled through, looking like a little mummy with snow-white gauze and surgical tape tightly swaddling her head.

About a week after the crash, LaDonna's father broke the bad news about the rest of the family and gently asked the preschooler what she could remember. The traumatized child responded with unexpected calm.

"Daddy," LaDonna whispered from beneath her bandages, "the angels came and got them." That's all she recalled.

## No Divine Help Wanted

TODAY, CASUAL contact with LaDonna—a petite, forty-something hairstylist with dark Italian good looks—would lend few clues about the emotional and spiritual junkyards she's had to pick through. With a reconstructed nose and multiple skin grafts, her face reveals only a faint trace of the day the freight train thundered over her family so many years ago. The incest and neglect that tainted her teen years with guilt and shame also linger only as ghosts too sheer for others to see.

Instead, friends and salon clients pick up on LaDonna's wisecracking personality and boisterous laugh. Her spunky attitude buoys her blues—and theirs—most of the time. Fact is, for decades LaDonna barely peeked at her past and even more rarely shared that glimpse with others. Why? What good would it do? She preferred to work hard and forget it with white knuckles and pursed lips.

When socially acceptable avoidance tactics failed— doomed from the start like all strategies aimed at pacifying symptoms rather than addressing causes—she inevitably resorted to an arsenal of destructive distractions. She slept with a series of Romeos, guzzled alcohol, and puffed joints and snorted cocaine on the weekends.

But when these classic quick fixes brought her to the very edge of insanity, she panicked and switched gears to bodybuilding, clay sculpting, inner child seminars—you name it. During this time, her healthiest coping method involved attending a weekly Tuesday night ACoA (Adult Children of Alcoholics/Dysfunctional Families) support group.

Even there, though, she managed to trudge through the twelve-step program for four years without tipping her hat to any higher power. Phrases like "Let go, and let God" continued to alienate her. Though quietly driven by unresolved pain and emptiness, she vowed to try anything— as long as God wasn't in it.

## THE CHEMISTRY OF REJECTION

DO YOU know anybody like LaDonna? Unless you live a cloistered life populated only with card-carrying church folks, you will meet people like her on every mile of your journey. Yet, though Christ pours extra effort into reaching the LaDonnas of the world, His people often noticeably pull back. Those hostile to the gospel exert power—a power strong enough to cause many Christians to deep-six the very thought of a divine appointment.

After all, even letting the Holy Spirit orchestrate meetings with seemingly neutral people—friends, siblings, coworkers, or neighbors—strikes some as an extreme faith adventure. Add negative vibes to the mix, and the chemistry of rejection seems sure and explosive.

Without understanding all the reasons why someone has rejected Jesus Christ or why that person could ultimately accept Him, you may feel your availability shrink ten sizes in five seconds. It seems like any goodwill gesture will backfire. Why should you continue to care and to look for ways to share your faith when someone tunes out, changes the subject, or cops a been-there-heard-that attitude of disdain?

No wonder plenty of believers mumble "pass" when the Holy Spirit arranges face time with characters like LaDonna. These believers mistakenly assume that such anti-faith decisions are done deals—that nothing they can do or say will break the ice and encourage that person to find God or walk more closely with Him. Those indifferent, defensive, or hostile to the gospel seem to need a divine appointment with an angel, not a mere mortal. After all, that's what it took to knock Paul off his horse and bring him to his knees on the Damascus road.

However, doesn't this response reflect a subtle pride, a backdoor attempt at playing God? In writing off this type of opportunity as "Mission Impossible," you trump the Holy Spirit. It's like you know best who belongs in God's kingdom based on who appears to be the most likely candidate.

## SOFTENING HARDENED HEARTS

THE PROBLEM is that you can't see what the Spirit sees. You will seldom know precisely why someone gives God the cold shoulder or angrily shakes a fist at Him. But there's probably a story—probably many stories—that explain each callus on a hard heart.

Think of the staunchest unbelievers you've met. If you don't understand the rest of that person's story, his or her chilly response to faith may choke your compassion, deflate your hope, and amply supply you with excuses to avoid expressing God's love in word and deed. But who can predict how prayer, love, and genuine friendship—along with goodwill tangibles like a jar of jelly, a pound of coffee, or a loaf of homemade bread—can soften even the crustiest folks?

Besides missing ministry opportunities, the believer

who always shrinks before the ardent skeptic also shrinks from identifying with the way Christ acted toward tough cases. He experienced rejection despite living a sin-free life and demonstrating His power through many miracles and unconditional love. Did He shake off His sandals in disgust? Did He lose hope and give up? No. Without forcing anyone's hand, Christ remained bent on seeking and saving the lost. Regardless of a person's troubled history or unwelcoming response to Him, Jesus continued ministering with compassion.

## Compassion's Call

SURELY, THE bottomless depth of Christ's no-strings-attached compassion comes from His omniscience—His ability to know all. How else could He stand to approach our brokenness and rebellion with tenderness instead of wrath? He knows *exactly* why those unmoved by the gospel need every ounce of His love and compassion.

Likewise, if you could read the rest of every unbeliever's story before meeting him or her—if you knew the specific reasons that left that person disappointed by God or bitterly wondering why He allows suffering—it could revolutionize your ministry. Namely, by grasping why someone feels justified in rejecting God, you could more easily appreciate what it would take to turn that perception around.

But that's the catch. Divine appointments rarely take place in ideal environments—like a psychiatrist's quiet office. In this controlled setting, the unbeliever would relax on a leather couch to candidly share his fears and insecurities about God while you skim his neatly typed case study. In reality, you might stumble into an opportunity while perusing the paper during your subway commute or

45

cheering at your daughter's swim meet or jump-starting a stalled mini-van in the middle of a blizzard.

It's as if God mysteriously puts people on your radar screen. From 1955 to 1957, my father served as a radar technician in the U.S. Army. He stayed on as a repairman at the Aberdeen Proving Grounds school in Maryland, where he worked in a lab where students used radar screens to practice guided missile exercises. That picture sticks with him as a divine-appointments metaphor not because he wants to blow up the unbeliever, but because he wants to detect them when they cross his path.

Circumstances rarely allow you to gather helpful cause-and-effect information about where people are coming from. They just step into view. So perhaps the most critical aspect of being ready and willing to keep divine appointments 24/7 with someone like LaDonna means asking God to give you the heart of Jesus. When this happens, be prepared for colossal changes in your point of view.

Why? God's heart transplants, at least the ones that take, beat with compassion—the hallmark of Jesus' ministry. He showed this quality on nearly every occasion, regardless of how inappropriate it seemed. Do you think the robber nailed to the cross next to His expected compassion, much less the promise of paradise?

What about the woman at the well? In her shame, she lied about her current husband and the string of other men she had married and divorced. She tried to hide her past because she anticipated being slammed with judgment and scorn. Then she glanced into Jesus' eyes and the truth came out. What was the point of covering up? His quiet compassion overpowered her concerns about being harshly treated with prejudice, fear, legalism, or scorn. This scene is no place for a white-knuckled Christian.

## ENTER GENTLE BETTY

MY MOTHER never attended seminary, but she keeps the tightest grip on solid theology—that God doesn't shudder before unbelief and that He's faithful in arranging divine appointments. Good thing! When in 1983 she first took a seat at the upscale hair salon where LaDonna worked, she quickly noticed how conversations that turned to God silenced the otherwise bubbly stylist. But that doesn't stop my mom. Icy responses to her faith in God actually warm her heart. It's like she's got compassion as a sixth sense. Besides, persistence seems inextricably woven into our family's genetic code.

She simply appreciates that those with the greatest resistance to God often have the greatest need for Him and often make His greatest road warriors. With this attitude, she marks the most challenging divine appointments as the most promising.

This insight motivates her to show compassion and concern for others *regardless* of whether she knows all the compelling reasons why they try to avoid God the way Christians try to avoid red-light districts. In any case, avoidance is an easy way to sidestep truth that may change a status-quo behavior or belief. That was certainly true in LaDonna's case.

"I didn't want to hear one little bit about God," LaDonna admits. The rest of her story amply explains why she felt so strongly. But when my mom met her, she couldn't begin to guess it. She hadn't been briefed! But the Lord knew LaDonna's past, just like He knew the background of the woman at the well. And He knew that my mom would be showing up at LaDonna's station every Friday for thirty minutes year after year. Some would call this arrangement a complete coincidence, but we see God calling Mom to show her availability and exercise her faith.

To that end, my mom and gifted evangelists like her are really just like you. They must watch their radar screens for divine appointments and walk by faith alone. To do so, invite the Holy Spirit to fill you and tenderize your heart without any foreknowledge of why. Let Him take you by the hand and then trust Him to lead you through that person's minefield of hurts and disappointments. Along the way, you may be able to fill in the missing pieces. But, by that time, it won't matter as much because your heart's been in the right spot all along.

## THE REST OF LADONNA'S STORY

IT TOOK my mother twelve years to lead LaDonna to Christ. LaDonna now confesses that she dreaded dealing with this "God lady" who wore her faith on her sleeve. Yet she dutifully listened—sometimes with wary openness and other times with a granite front of frustration—from the shampoo to the finishing mist of hairspray. Then, when my mother left with her new coiffure, LaDonna shook off all that talk about God like a puppy shakes off bath water.

Who would suspect the kind of baggage LaDonna carried, the reasons why she might consider God cruel and distant? From my mom's limited perspective, LaDonna appeared to be a "with it" woman. She dressed fashionably, socialized effortlessly with all types of people, and ranked as the priciest, most popular stylist in town.

With that image in play, no one would ever picture her as a shy, preadolescent girl compulsively studying disfiguring facial scars in the mirror. Who could guess how grotesque and utterly unlovable LaDonna felt before her reflection? Plastic surgery would smooth her skin, making her face a trophy in her surgeon's practice. But changing how she looked failed to change much about how she felt. She still suffered flashbacks of the accident, and those emotional wounds never healed.

So with no one to tell her anything different, the pre-teen LaDonna ultimately blamed God for the train wreck. After she healed from eight consecutive cosmetic operations and developed into a young woman, she found herself fending off sexual advances from a family member and suffering indifference to her pleas for protection. Her hurt and anger ballooned.

"I just thought nobody but nobody was there for me," LaDonna reflects. This may explain some of the sharp, hair-raising turns she took over the next two decades. For instance, at age sixteen she got pregnant and started living with her boyfriend in a slum section in a nearby town. After two months of crashing on the floor and rattling empty cupboards for food, she felt desperate—desperate enough to take her stepmother's advice and abort her baby. When she sought professional counseling for the first time at age twenty-eight, she realized that she had never talked about these traumas—much less shed a tear.

## THE TURNING POINT

NOT SURPRISINGLY, the root of LaDonna's unrest with God started when that train wouldn't stop. Without faith, she seemed forever unable to come to terms with the mess of it and move forward. Yet, like others who find Christ as adults, she realized that she could only harbor that grudge so long. Her heart tired from being so defiantly at odds with its Maker and, frankly, nothing in three decades of experimentation had helped her heal.

Through twelve years of weekly hair appointments and my parents' fervent prayers, LaDonna seemed a confirmed spiritual cipher—a woman destined to wander without Christ forever. No evidence pointed to the contrary. But as the calendar pages turned through the four seasons again and again, all those low-key contacts with Mom eventually blossomed into a mentoring relationship.

The turning point took place one day as LaDonna routinely trimmed and teased my mom's short salt-and-pepper hair. When she nonchalantly started asking about Jesus—that name that was off-limits for so long—my mom struggled to keep her composure. What a joy it was to witness LaDonna searching for answers in God's direction.

"There was a point where all I wanted to do was get out of bed to turn on the car and commit suicide," LaDonna says, recalling the desperate final days of her life as an unbeliever. Instead, my mom invited her to hear the testimony of a former drug addict and drug runner—you guessed it, Bryan Marcoux, the wild Mafia guy mentioned in chapter 1. He spoke in the family-room addition we built on our home to hold seventy people for these kind of outreaches, a welcoming space in which dozens have accepted Christ. After revealing his own brokenness and explaining the effects of Christ's healing touch, Bryan introduced the sinner's prayer and invited the group to repeat it after him if they felt so led.

"That's it," LaDonna remembers thinking with resignation. "I'm going to do it. I'm going to allow Christ into my life, and I'm going to just see what happens. I'm letting You in, God. Now, You tell me You're here."

## UNSOLVED MYSTERIES AND UNEXPECTED MIRACLES

BELIEVE IT or not, LaDonna had been toying with the idea of submitting the story of her accident to the *Unsolved Mysteries* television show in hopes of tracking relatives on her mother's side—people she had lost contact with after the funerals. Specifically, she wanted to find her maternal grandfather and her mother's other sister, a woman she had never met.

After LaDonna accepted Christ on something of a trial basis, she woke up at 1 A.M. and sensed Him urging her to write the letter. Feelings of foolishness dogged her. Yet she wrote it before switching off the light, and she mailed it that morning. As soon as the heavy steel pull-down door slammed and her letter floated to the bottom of the mailbox, she regretted the action. But it was too late. A month later, the show's producer called and arranged to tape a seven-minute dramatization of the tragedy. When that clip aired with a contact number for tipsters, LaDonna nervously paced in the California studio beside a long telephone bank of thirty phones.

The operators could have gone out to dinner when the show aired on the East Coast. An hour later, it aired in the Midwest and produced a jingle here and there. That's when LaDonna gravely started coming to terms with the emptiness of her hopes. Then, in a swift reversal of fortune, callers jammed the circuits. Her grandfather finally got through from his home in Sioux Falls, South Dakota, after several attempts.

As a follow-up to this breakthrough, the show flew LaDonna to South Dakota from Connecticut for an upcoming family reunion. In this way, after a thirty-year communication blackout, LaDonna got a closer look at her mother's family for the first time and was hugged by someone who really loved her.

After the four-day reunion, she and her grandfather strolled together to her gate at the airport. That's when the eighty-six-year-old man shared that he had prayed for years for a chance to see her before he died, including the night before *Unsolved Mysteries* aired.

"Really?" LaDonna said.

"God strike me dead," he responded with a laugh.

"Don't you dare!" she shouted. "I just found you."

In an unbelievable turn of events, her grandfather passed away just hours later, before LaDonna reached her door in New England. Yet this sad part of her story reinforced her burgeoning faith. It dawned on her that God may have orchestrated this meeting to reveal Himself and, in this way, to answer her prayer. For the first time, she began making peace with the tough concepts of both unsolved mysteries and unexpected miracles.

## THE REST OF BRYAN'S STORY

IN LADONNA'S case, my mother had to wait more than ten years to lead her to Christ and to at last learn the rest of her story—the reasons behind her staunch anti-God beliefs and behaviors. However, not all divine appointments require this kind of patience and unfaltering hope. Remember Bryan, the ex-Mafia man my mom led to Christ in our kitchen mere hours after making his acquaintance (the same guy who led LaDonna to accept Christ in our living room)? At that time, my mom knew nothing of his role in organized crime, nothing of his X-rated past, nothing of his spiritual condition. All she could see was a big, tough guy—in his own words, a "punk." Yet she operated under the assumption that the rest of his story would bear out why he rejected Christ—and why he ultimately accepted Him.

So when you don't know the rest of the story, remember that it's okay to act like you do—at least in the general sense. Why? Because Luke 4:18 stresses that everyone, whether they realize it or not, struggles with a broken heart, spiritual blindness and bruises, or bondage to Satan.

In Bryan's case, his contempt for God cropped up when he reached age thirteen. He grew up in a healthy, churchgoing family in Prospect, Connecticut. But at a critical point in his development, he felt the judgment—not the love—of the church. So he bolted and never looked back.

His disillusionment happened shortly after his parents gave him a .22 rifle on his thirteenth birthday. Before shooting it, he attended National Rifle Association safety classes and eagerly awaited his first hunting trip. Meanwhile, he invited his friend Jay to join him at a nearby reservoir for target practice.

During one of those sessions, a bullet from Bryan's gun ricocheted off the pavement. The freak accident caused the stray bullet to burrow up Jay's nose and push his right eyeball forward before lodging near his temple—half an inch away from killing him. Amazingly, Jay remained conscious and fled home.

The surgeon who treated the gunshot wound opted to leave the bullet untouched, so to this day Jay's nickname is "Lead Head." For years, kids also called Bryan "Double O 22." Despite the prey-and-predator overtones to their nicknames, the boys remained friends and eventually resumed practicing their sport. However, during the early stages of Jay's recovery, Bryan worried incessantly and struggled to regroup under the glare of disapproving adults—men and women who wrongly assumed that he had meant to hurt his friend.

## THE PAST'S REACH

WHEN BRYAN attended church a week after the accident, he realized that nasty rumors had spread through the congregation, vilifying him as a thwarted murderer.

Instead of showing compassion to a very shaken boy with grief and regret on his conscience, members whispered behind his back.

"That broke my heart," Bryan explains. "And I never went back to church again."

A week after that crisis, Bryan got more bad news. His older high-school-aged brother, while driving between eighty and one hundred miles per hour on a drug rush, had wrapped his car around a telephone pole. While townspeople visited the family's home to express regrets, Bryan hunched on the curb watching traffic pass and sourly thinking, *If there is a God, He can just kiss off.*

Two days later, at his brother's wake, Bryan started smoking marijuana because his brother's friends told him that weed would make him feel better. Long term, it made him feel worse because it shredded the concentration he needed for school and distracted him from honestly addressing and constructively resolving his most pressing personal problems.

Instead, more anger roiled inside him like hot lava. Eventually, Bryan filled the void in his heart—that really big space where God fits—with racist hatred, a fast-lane lifestyle in organized crime, and drug-induced highs, all to no avail.

The past most certainly informs the present. Had my mother known Bryan's history, she probably would have weighed the importance of her divine appointment with him a little more heavily. She could have geared their conversation to a more specific agenda. But she didn't need to know the rest of his story to show compassion. She just assumed that something big back there had brought him here, to a kitchen table conversation about God and His power to forgive. Like a Secret Service agent, she did her little part without the benefit of knowing the big picture.

## NO TRESPASSING?

AT SOME point, if you're open enough, God will put people like LaDonna and Bryan in your path—people with tough pasts that act as roadblocks to believers. They may hang "No Trespassing" and "Keep Out" notices in every area of their lives. But a believer available for divine appointments should view those postings as a different kind of sign. The warnings may be more accurately read as, "Proceed with Caution If Carrying Good News."

Approaching this type of person requires unconditional compassion and one more ingredient—curiosity. Together, compassion and curiosity will lead you down some roads overgrown with thistles and washed out by countless floods. But eventually, you find yourself in a clearing with a house and an occupant inside. At this point, the "No Trespassing" signs are spray-painted on old cars parked for decades in the front yard. As you get closer, you notice more-threatening epitaphs—like "Trespassers Will Be Shot"—nailed to nearby walnut trees.

Worse, when you reach the porch, old whiskey bottles are lying there along with animal skulls and vats of suspect black liquid. Other than the tattered plastic fluttering over the jagged holes in the twelve-pane windows, it's quiet as a morgue.

Rap on the door, and the moment of truth opens. You wince and wait for the immediate future to unfold. Eventually, you figure no one's home and release a sigh mixed with equal parts of disappointment and relief. As you gingerly step down the creaky, weather-beaten steps, the door's rusty hinges squeak as someone slowly pushes it open.

"What do you want!" a gaunt man bellows from the shadowy interior. "Can't you read the signs?"

"Just had to see who lived back here," you stammer.

"Yeah, well. Now you know," he grumbles and tugs both hooks on his faded bib overalls. "Maybe I need to put up more signs—in fluorescent orange, pink, green, and yellow."

"I guess so," you mutter. "But I figured anyone living back here behind all these signs must have a story."

"A story!" the grizzled man sputters. "Whaddya mean, a 'story'? Yeah, I got a story all right."

"Let's hear it," you entreat, cautiously easing up the swaybacked steps.

When the old man squints in the afternoon sun, it deepens the wrinkles that run over his face like berserk tributaries without a main river. His voice sounds passive as he shares how he toiled to earn a living off all three hundred acres of this plot. Once, he hired a neighbor kid to cut corn with him. The men were down at the far end of the field when the neighbor kid hopped off the tractor to remove a sapling stretched across a row. That's when the machine somehow popped back into gear and crushed the young man, killing him instantly.

"I know those folks back in town blame me and my drinkin', but heck, I wasn't even drinkin' that day," the former farmer muses sadly.

"What folks back in town?" you ask.

"Oh, old man Harlock and that whole gang," he replies.

"Mr. Harlock died over thirty years ago, when I was a kid," you point out. "Have you been to town recently?"

"Heck no! Last time I went in, they threw rocks at my truck. Looky there. You can still see the dents on my hood," he says, pointing to an old relic with no tires. "Parked right there when I got back here safely. Keys are still in it."

"Mister? Why all the 'No Trespassing' signs?" you abruptly question.

"Errr . . . ahhh . . . well, I guess it was easier for me to just hide out here till the whole thing, the accident with the kid, blew over. Got me a garden back yonder and plenty of squirrels around. Even got a stove for them long winter nights."

After a stretch of silence, you mention something about the sun sinking and getting home in time for supper. Bidding him adieu, you amble back to your car. A ball of mayflies dances ten paces ahead and, above, geese honk out their report. Before disappearing into the overgrown thicket and deep woods, you glance over your shoulder to see the old man unpinning his clean clothes from the line.

The Spirit of God has turned a day studded with threatening signs into a divine appointment, albeit one of the most preliminary kind. No matter. Equipped with compassion and curiosity, you know you'll be back to hear the rest of his story—and perhaps, to share the rest of God's story too.

# KEEPING
## APPOINTMENTS

1. Betty Jacks shared her faith with LaDonna Alfano for twelve years before LaDonna trusted Christ. How did Betty find the necessary patience, persistence, and hope?

2. When should you "give up" on reaching out to an unbeliever?

3. What would it take to help the unbelievers in your world recognize their need for Christ?

4. Can God use believers like Bryan and LaDonna in ways He can't use you? Why?

5. Bryan was turned off to God by the church. Is your church a "safe" place for people who don't have it all put together? Why or why not?

6. Bob and Betty work as a team to reach out—like adding onto their house to reach people who may feel uncomfortable attending church, or praying for people in their world. Do you have a team member? What qualities do you like in a team member?

7. Like the old man at the end of this chapter, do wounded people often prop up "No Trespassing" signs? If so, how do you get permission to step into their lives? Do you trust the Holy Spirit for guidance in these situations?

# CHAPTER FOUR

# GETTING EQUIPPED

### BY BOB JACKS

*The church ceases to be a spiritual society when it is on the lookout for the development of its own organization.*

—OSWALD SANDERS, *MY UTMOST FOR HIS HIGHEST,* JULY 12

*Now to him who is able to do immeasurably more than all we ask or imagine, according to his power that is at work within us . . .*

—EPHESIANS 3:20

∾  ∾  ∾

ONE FROSTY SUNDAY MORNING in January, my pastor, Dr. Jay Abramson, dusted off history and talked about the evidence that turned up when researchers ordered Ludwig van Beethoven's body exhumed. For nearly two centuries, causes of the composer's deafness and death presented a question mark. Now, at last, high-tech DNA testing would unlock the secret.

From just one strand of hair and some orthodontia, scientists determined that both his heartbreaking hearing loss beginning at age thirty and his death at age fifty-seven stemmed from lead poisoning. Turns out that Beethoven may have regularly submerged in tainted hot springs to relax and rejuvenate, exposing himself to sky-high levels of the toxin. Ironically, he would have regarded these steamy baths as therapy good for both body and soul.

Anyone lulled into a quiet repose by his haunting Moonlight Sonata or enraptured by his Symphony no. 5 as it thunders along, measure after measure, enjoys what he could not. Though he composed for the rest of his life, Beethoven went stone deaf by age forty.

# THE "HOLY" HOT TUB

LIKE BEETHOVEN, you may seek comfort and strength in warm, seemingly therapeutic places. But you don't need dips in a lead-tainted pool to suffer compromised health from overexposure—even to good things. For instance, a little bit of sunshine helps the human body manufacture vitamin D. Days full of sunshine start outweighing that benefit by prematurely aging the skin and increasing the risk of skin cancer.

Nevertheless, plenty of well-meaning believers slip into church or parachurch organizations with as much relief and contentment as Beethoven slipped into his gently circulating mineral waters. Why not? At face value, a holy hot tub experience—sitting in a ring bubbling with warmth and heartfelt consensus among believers—seems like a wonderful idea. For the most part, it is.

There you'll get guidance, structure, and support to help you build a stronger relationship with God. Regular contact with your pastor and the congregation will hopefully deepen your trust in Christ and encourage your personal growth. But ultimately, your church's worship, teaching, and cozy fellowship should motivate you to get spiritually fit and stay limber enough to exercise your faith in harsher conditions.

Not surprisingly, prolonged immersion experiences in the holy hot tub can make you go soft on reaching a broken world with the claims of Christ. Like Beethoven, you may not be aware of the bath's potent quality—even as your vitality quietly drains away. So while making the holy hot tub scene as inviting and nurturing as possible, God's people need to be extra-intentional about equipping themselves to meet unbelievers in uncharted waters. You can bet these places won't be ringed with decorative mosaic tile, filled with climate-controlled water, and bobbing with kindred spirits.

## PURPOSEFULLY PRESENT

MAKING A total commitment to Christ and considering others with His compassion—the subjects of chapters 2 and 3—fundamentally factor into the equipping process. Another giant step is to deliberately put yourself in the path of divine appointments.

Chris and Alice Canlis own a popular, well-established family restaurant in Seattle. Recognizing that they were living too far from the spiritual front, they took steps to get closer to it. For them, this in part meant pulling their children out of private Christian schools and enrolling them in public schools. They felt their children were ready to face a spiritually diverse setting that would stretch the entire family's faith. Attending public school extracurricular activities would give them another convenient opportunity to mingle with unbelieving parents. And it was all prompted because the Canlises were serious about keeping divine appointments and decided to be intentional in making them happen. When equipped believers deliberately foster this mindset and presence—in whatever form it takes—you can sooner or later expect population shifts between those who call Jesus Lord and those who don't.

In *The God Chasers,* Tommy Tenney outlines the potential power of this kind of purposeful presence:

> We understand "program evangelism," where we knock on doors or pass out tracts, or some other program of the church designed to reach the lost. John Wimber helped us to understand "power evangelism," where we mix anointing with the

program. In this form of evangelism, we might pray for someone to be healed on the street instead of just witnessing or giving out tracts. But there is a little understood, much underused form of evangelism that I call "presence evangelism." This is where [unbelievers] take note, saying, "They have been with Jesus" (see Acts 4:13). This is when the residue of God on a person creates a divine radiation zone of the manifest presence of God, so much that it affects those around you.[1]

## FELLOWSHIP CITY AND SATANSVILLE

THE CATCH is that both good and evil find ways to manifest themselves. So besides recognizing the isolating potential of the Christian subculture and the separation that often ensues, getting equipped also involves recognizing spiritual warfare. I lump the two spiritual forces into opposing camps I call "Fellowship City" and "Satansville."

Satansville sounds like an unattractive destination, and it is. Yet Jesus visited often. If you follow Him, so will you. Luke 4:18 (KJV) states the mission: "He hath sent me to heal the brokenhearted, to preach deliverance to the captives, and recovering of sight to the blind, to set at liberty them that are bruised." Being brokenhearted, captive, blind, or bruised is Satan's handiwork. The key is not to focus on Satan and his deeds but to keep your eyes on Christ.

Much as Jesus calls believers to disperse throughout Satansville as salt and light, He recognizes the perils of getting caught in a cosmic Star Wars–like spiritual battle. As recorded in Matthew 10:16, He put the conflict in simple terms: "I am sending you out like sheep among wolves. Therefore be as shrewd as snakes and as innocent as doves." Like it or not, this reality surrounds every divine appointment.

In *Against the Night*, Charles Colson writes,

> The forces of evil have begun their decisive offensive. You can feel their pressure, yet your screens and publications are full of prescribed smiles and raised glasses. What is the joy about?
> . . . Can the new barbarians be resisted? But even if they cannot, we must go forward in obedience, in hope, even joy. For those who are "signed of the cross of Christ go gaily in the dark."[2]

During the summer of 1996, I understood spiritual warfare more clearly than ever as I led seminars in Kiev, Ukraine. Sharing the Your Home a Lighthouse movement Betty and I had developed in the United States made me especially vulnerable. After all, my job involved equipping others, which exponentially increased the potential number of people reached with the gospel—and my vulnerability to Satan's attacks.

## No Disney World

THE AWARENESS of the dark forces conspiring against me in Kiev arose when I met two stylishly dressed men in the lobby of the small church-run hotel. They were waiting for my host, Victor Branitski, an evangelist and the president of Slavic Ministries, because they wanted him to deliver a personal message to one of their friends in prison.

One man, Valeriy, stood with the aid of crutches, his left leg amputated up to his hip. His companion spoke broken English, so I attempted to make small talk by inquiring about their line of work as we waited for Victor. They offered only evasive answers. Later Victor told me that these two, along with another accomplice, single-handedly controlled Kiev's underworld for a number of years.

A few evenings later, Valeriy showed up at my seminar with his girlfriend. Neither had any genuine interest in my seminar. They appeared only to petition Victor to deliver another message to their friend behind bars. Because he was busy interpreting for me, they got stuck waiting until after the session to speak with him.

Before I started speaking, Valeriy insisted on sharing how he had witnessed a double murder while playing poker. Victor translated the story for me in a low voice. Evidently, one player had embarrassed another player. Besides blushing, the humiliated one pulled out a pistol and killed the offender and the unlucky man seated near him. Though the murderer landed in prison, I nervously wondered what kind of character I had on my hands that night.

Surprisingly, Valeriy and his girlfriend sat in the front row not two feet from me, with a small table between us. After the first ten minutes of listening to my message, they started playing a little game with a decorative vase and plastic flower decorating the table. They slid it back and forth like two hockey players without sticks. Soon I was speaking to the walls because all eyes were on this match, especially when they started playing more aggressively. At that point, without thinking, I reached down and snatched the vase. That's when Valeriy angrily repeated a snippet of his story—how a man had shot two others out of embarrassment.

Fear gripped me like it has only gripped me a couple of other times before, and I immediately recognized the spiritual warfare taking place in that room. While I tried to spread the good news to others who would do likewise through home Bible studies, this guy had parked right under my nose and challenged me with an evil, intimidating stare for the duration of the seminar. Afterward I left without mingling to prevent him from trailing me to my room. I then shoved a dresser up against the door, prayed for protection, and trusted my prayer network back home to cover me as well.

Later Valeriy killed the doctor whom he resented for amputating his leg—even though the surgery saved his life—and the doctor's wife. He seems an unlikely candidate for a divine appointment. Or does he? God performs miracles by divine appointment. During one of Victor's recent visits to Ukraine, he led Valeriy's best friend to Christ. Who knows? Maybe Victor's next opportunity will be with Valeriy himself.

## PROTECTIVE GEAR

IN SPIRITUAL contests between Fellowship City and Satansville, all believers face depressing shortcomings. By the time this book gets published, I'll be seventy years old. I don't have many regrets, but I'll confess that I've always desired to play in the National Football League. The trouble is that I couldn't have been born any more poorly equipped for that job. Even if I had winged feet, a good head for football, and a sticky grip, I lacked physical heft. During my college days, I was five feet ten and weighed 128 pounds—runt material on a college football team, much less the pros.

The fact is, when you prepare for divine appointments, you must allow Jesus Christ to make your little much. However, this act of submission and trust doesn't mean that you scrap spring training. You still need your playbook, your personal trainer, scrimmaging opportunities, and proper protective gear to get equipped for long-haul availability.

In Ephesians 6:10-18, Paul explained why this gear is critical and how to put it on:

Finally, be strong in the Lord and in his mighty power. Put on the full armor of God so that you can take your stand against the devil's schemes. For our struggle is not against flesh and blood, but against the rulers, against the authorities, against the powers of this dark world and against the spiritual forces of evil in the heavenly realms. Therefore put on the full armor of God, so that when the day of evil comes, you may be able to stand your ground, and after you have done everything, to stand. Stand firm then, with the belt of truth buckled around your waist, with the breastplate of righteousness in place, and with your feet fitted with the readiness that comes from the gospel of peace. In addition to all this, take up the shield of faith, with which you can extinguish all the flaming arrows of the evil one. Take the helmet of salvation and the sword of the Spirit, which is the word of God. And pray in the Spirit on all occasions with all kinds of prayers and requests. With this in mind, be alert and always keep on praying for all the saints.

## MOTHER TERESA GETS DRESSED

SUCH INVISIBLE "suiting up" causes some of the most petite people to weigh in as Goliaths for God. Bill Bright recalls a story about Mother Teresa:

A dear friend, Dee Jepsen, wife of former U.S. Senator Roger Jepsen, attended a luncheon in the Senate Caucus Room on Capitol Hill in Washington, D.C. Congressmen, Cabinet members, top leaders in government and many other respected guests were seated in the impressive room with its ornate pillars, high ceilings and huge chandeliers. The room seemed to swell with influential people who had gathered to honor a humble servant of God.

Then Mother Teresa entered the room.

Mrs. Jepsen said, "She looked so tiny and out-of-place in her blue-and-white habit, old gray sweater and sandals that had obviously carried her many miles. The room and prestigious guests seemed to dwarf her."

Immediately the top leaders of the most powerful country in the world along with the other esteemed guests rose to their feet and applauded. Many had tears in their eyes.

"I was struck with the contrast," Mrs. Jepsen said. "I thought, 'Lord, this frail woman has more power than I see in the Halls of Congress. She reflects Jesus everywhere she goes, and everyone is strangely moved.'"

"Mother Teresa doesn't own anything," Bright writes.

She has never asked for material possessions nor held up her fist to demand rights for herself. Yet she has been raised to a pinnacle of recognition for her work with the destitute and dying in Calcutta, India. She has reached down into the gutter and loved those whom the world has called unlovable. A shining example of selfless-ness, she proves the power of God's love to transform people and touch a starved world.[3]

I still recall televangelist Robert Schuller's interview with Mother Teresa on his *Hour of Power* program. When he asked what her prayer for him would be, she calmly responded, "I would ask the Lord Jesus to use you without your permission."

## SPIRITUAL BREATHING

THE REMARKABLE purity and focus of Mother Teresa's obedience also stemmed from how she used prayer to get equipped for ministry. For instance, every day she approached God with cycles of confessing sin and praying for forgiveness. Bright calls this powerful equipping discipline "spiritual breathing."

"To 'exhale' spiritually, confess any known sin in your life," Bright recommends.

> God's Word promises in 1 John 1:9, "If we confess our sins, he is faithful and just and will forgive us our sins and purify us from all unrighteousness." By confession, you agree with God that your action is sinful and therefore grievous to him; you acknowledge that Christ has paid the penalty for your sin; then you repent by turning away from your wrongdoing.

"To 'inhale' spiritually, simply appropriate the fullness of God's Spirit by faith," he adds. "Invite Him to direct, control and empower your life according to His promises in Acts 1:8."[4] That Scripture reads, "But you will receive power when the Holy Spirit comes on you; and you will be my witnesses in Jerusalem, and in all Judea and Samaria, and to the ends of the earth."

# THE LITTLE GUYS

JESUS TOOK sin seriously because sin separates us from Him and often rusts personal and organizational ministry like an old Chevy—from the inside out. Yet how many people underestimate the power of sin? Dana Carvey's *Saturday Night Live* "Church Lady" skits touched on this disbelief by tickling audiences with the feather of a partial truth. In it he portrayed a paranoid little old religious lady who, when faced with problems, predictably chirped, "Could it be Satan?"

Surely some believers overspiritualize trials and tribulations. They scapegoat Satan as the crafty one who has engineered every roadblock in their lives. But to go to the other extreme, and not take Satan and sin seriously, is even more dangerous.

Getting equipped for divine appointments must be infused with a keen awareness of sin. Satan is not a fairy-tale figure, the ultimately redeemable and lovable Grinch who stole Christmas. Rather, the Bible describes him as a roaring lion seeking someone to devour (see 1 Peter 5:8). He's got teeth and a big appetite for believers.

Jesus recommends cutting off your right hand if it offends you with sin (see Matthew 5:30). But don't haul out the machete just yet. In this passage, He's really calling you to surrender anything that hinders your relationship with Him or others. The biggies are obvious—substance abuse, illicit sexual relationships, white-collar theft, and the like. Then there are those sins my friend Dave Findley calls the "respectable sins" or the "little guys."

# THE BASICS

FOR WEEKS now, Dave and I have been coteaching a class based on an anonymously written book, *How to Live the Victorious Life.* Many class members are new believers with scant equipping, so we gear our message to the seeker and the new believer. The book gives us a platform to review the basics—for instance, that sin hobbles a believer's walk with Christ and that unconfessed sin "de-equips" like nothing else.

"Remember Aretha Franklin's theme song?" Dave began class one night while flipping his dry-board marker up in the air. "R-E-S-P-E-C-T," he sang in falsetto while clowning the sassy singer's stage performance. Some sins demand respect the way she did—even when they don't necessarily deserve it. But so-called respectable sins don't flagrantly break the Ten Commandments or any governmental laws. Gossip, white lies, insincere flattery, laziness, gluttony, pride, and jealousy all qualify as respectable sins. And who would ever know if you occasionally checked out an X-rated Internet site or fudged on your business expense records?

Rationalizations sound embarrassingly familiar: Everyone does it. It's only human. You can't get arrested for it. Our class sheepishly smiled as Dave rattled off the list. But then he pivoted on his heel and explained why respectable sins rank right up there with all the sins that blink in neon.

"Respectable sins can easily become habits," he stated and paused a minute to scan the sixty faces turned his way. "When they become habits, we may not as easily recognize them. Without recognition, they can grow and become character shapers." If sin is the dominant influence in your life, it will hedge out Christ's influence and countless divine appointments with it.

## PAST THE "PREP" STEPS

TO RECAP, the key "prep" steps in getting equipped involve making a total commitment to Christ, considering others with compassion, recognizing the potential oil-and-water effect between believers and unbelievers, and finally, battling sin. The finer points of equipping come down to placing value on teaching, discipling, mentoring, serving, and worshiping.

~ *Teaching.* Paul wrote in 2 Timothy 3:16-17, "All Scripture is God-breathed and is useful for teaching, rebuking, correcting and training in righteousness, so that the man of God may be thoroughly equipped for every good work." Christ taught both Nicodemus and the crowd of five thousand. Your teaching can be done one on one or in a classroom. Regardless of setting, all teaching must be based on Scripture.

~ *Discipling.* Paul also wrote to Timothy, "And the things you have heard me say in the presence of many witnesses entrust to reliable men who will also be qualified to teach others" (2 Timothy 2:2). Discipleship involves putting all that you have learned together and sharing it with someone else. It is instruction. At 6 A.M. each Friday, I meet with a group of ten to fifteen men for this purpose. I also meet one on one with four other men once a week—two by long-distance telephone.

~ *Mentoring.* Mentoring is similar to discipleship. In *As Iron Sharpens Iron,* Howard and William Hendricks differentiate between the two:

> Mentoring, at least when practiced by Christians, certainly ought to center everything on Christ. But mentoring is less about instruction than it is about *initiation*—about bringing young men [and women too, I might add] into maturity. Whereas the word for disciple means "learner," the word *protégé* comes from a Latin word meaning "to protect." . . . The point is, we need older men and younger men *relating* in such a way that younger men grow as

older men guide. That is the historical pattern. It also happens to be the biblical pattern.[5]

∽ *Serving.* Teaching, discipling, and mentoring need to add up to serving in the field of resistance. To prepare for serving, I encourage others to write a five-minute testimony of their conversion experience or launch an evangelistic Bible study for unbelieving friends or disciple a new believer. Anyone serving in these ways will face resistance and that is exactly where spiritual growth and more substantive equipping happen.

∽ *Worshiping.* How, you may wonder, does worship equip someone for ministry? Worship will bring you closer to God. Besides worshiping at your local church, you may find ways to worship God in gatherings with thousands of people. This is the case when I attend the parachurch Vision New England conferences. Solitary worship can happen anywhere at any time. I often worship God best behind the wheel of my car. I pop in a praise CD and it helps me focus on Christ before I get wrapped up in the day's activities. Whatever the context, worship clears the clutter standing between you and God as well as between you and your next divine appointment.

I often get up between 2 and 5 A.M., sit on a comfortable couch, and pray about those things that seem to keep me awake: work-related challenges, finances, family issues, ministry opportunities, and a long list of nonbelievers in my world. This is a great worship experience for me.

# KEEPING
## APPOINTMENTS

1. How have some churches become the shelter Bob calls "Fellowship City"?

2. Has your church become too complacent about reaching out? If so, why? If not, what has kept it an equipping center? Give examples.

3. Do you agree that many believers don't know how unbelievers think? Why or why not?

4. Does Satan attack believers who share their faith in Christ? Why or why not?

5. Read Ephesians 6:10-18. Why did Paul write this letter?

6. Do you experience satanic oppression? If so, where does he usually start? How do you handle these situations?

7. Why is "spiritual breathing"—confessing your sins, receiving God's forgiveness, and appropriating the fullness of the Holy Spirit—so critical in a divine-appointments-oriented life?

# TEAM BUILDING

### BY BOB JACKS

*Our Lord implies that the only men and women He will use in His building enterprises are those who love Him personally, passionately, and devotedly beyond any of the closest ties on earth.*

—OSWALD CHAMBERS, *MY UTMOST FOR HIS HIGHEST*, MAY 7

*Some of them, . . . men from Cyprus and Cyrene, went to Antioch and began to speak to Greeks also, telling them the good news about the Lord Jesus. The Lord's hand was with them, and a great number of people believed and turned to the Lord. . . . [Barnabas, Paul's ministry partner] was a good man, full of the Holy Spirit and faith, and a great number of people were brought to the Lord.*

—ACTS 11:20-21,24

∿   ∿   ∿

TWELVE TIMES. KEVIN SEARLES' nagging hunches forced him to return to the Plainville, Connecticut, crime scene and interview twelve times in less than two weeks the woman who lived in the bungalow there. He meditated on her tone of voice, studied her gestures, and tried to catch her eyes. The truth lingered like the aroma of baking bread as they sat uncomfortably in her kitchen. It wafted everywhere but in her words.

Meanwhile, his precinct buddies back at the station shook their heads and threw up their hands in frustration. Why would a sharp detective like him waste so much time on a woman who repeated her story with believable rhetoric? Nothing suggested she knew who burglarized a home and five minutes later murdered the first cop who tried to prevent it that fall night in 1977.

The investigation stalled, and Kevin's boss considered his suspicions counterintuitive. No matter. Kevin snatched the thin file and burrowed into the investigation with more gusto. With wiretaps and steady surveillance, he watched this woman with an unblinking eye. Family, friends, and food all became second thoughts and dreams a memory as he restlessly slept at his office or in his car. If he waited long enough, he knew she'd tell the real story.

Kevin decided to grow old on the improbable case because the murdered policeman, Bob Holcumb, was his best friend and a big-brother figure as well as a pro at the Plainville Police Department. Dying like he did, in the line of duty, demanded justice. The problem was that with scant evidence, no one but Kevin thought it would ever be served.

Then, on Kevin's twelfth visit, the woman who had so cooly played cat-and-mouse with him ratted. With that name, the authorities at last closed in on the suspect later convicted as the killer.

## SPIRITUAL INKLINGS

AS A rookie detective, Kevin proved himself a quick study with an uncanny sixth sense. But long before he used those abilities to sleuth professionally, he started suspecting there was a God. Though his father hated God and disdained anyone who knew Him, Kevin couldn't shake his spiritual inklings. He held the stuff of student happiness in college. He enjoyed good grades, a fun part-time job, a great girlfriend, and plenty of pals. Yet, as he watched the western sky one sunset during his junior year, he sensed a black hole of emptiness that nothing else filled.

An emotional carbon copy of that melancholy epiphany returned during the next five years, most often on Sunday afternoons, regardless of if he was sitting on a bus heading back to school or later hanging out in the U.S. Army barracks. However, without a divine appointment, the altogether unchurched Kevin received few additional clues about Christ and His redemptive nature. So he just moved on with his life.

His rocky marriage finally broke up a year after the high-profile murder. That's when Kevin started dating an unlikely woman—Bob's widow, Nancy. The budding relationship surprised everyone, including them. Given the tangle of extenuating circumstances and the way they clashed before the tragedy, nobody gave the romance much of a chance. He thought the spunky, no-nonsense woman was controlling because she hadn't let Bob go out drinking with him and the boys. For her part, Nancy considered Kevin just another cocky young cop. Still, they must have seen in each other the qualities Bob once saw in them.

Neither mentioned wedding plans when they got an apartment together. Yet Nancy would soon question the live-in arrangement—to Kevin's chagrin. She rarely attended church and hadn't read her Bible in twenty-five years, but her husband's violent death had kindled her curiosity about God.

"I kept asking, 'Where is he?' I didn't mean, 'Where is Bob's body?' I meant, 'Where did Bob go?' because he died, and he didn't believe in Jesus," Nancy reflects. Others assured her that he landed in heaven—thanks to the good life he lived on earth. She showed up at one of our Bible studies looking for the truth.

## WARMING UP TO GOD

THAT YEAR, 1980, our friends and teammates—David and Helga Findley—were hosting evangelistic home Bible study outreaches. After a series of casual conversations about God, one of our teammates in that group invited Nancy to take another discovery step by joining her at the study.

The Findleys provided the venue, I led the discussion, and Betty remained available to help me answer any questions and to share informally during the refreshment time. About three months after I met Nancy, I was privileged to pray the sinner's prayer with her and welcome her into the family of Christ—good news she promptly took home to Kevin. When he finally agreed to attend the study with her, the strapping, steely-eyed guy arrived with his arms crossed and an eye on the clock.

"I was put off by the Bible study that Nancy was going to," Kevin admits. "I thought that they just wanted to run this religious scam by me. My father had trained me to think that all religious people were just after money. I remember when Bob asked me a few questions. I just gave terse answers. I did not want to get involved in this project." But deep down, Kevin was already warming up to this "God thing," something our team prayed for as we continued discipling Nancy.

When Kevin left his first Bible study, he swiped a paperback New Testament from the stack on the way out and read it from cover to cover during the next several days. Despite his tough exterior, he still fondly remembers the picture on the front of Jesus carrying a lamb on His shoulders. He also reluctantly attended a few more of the Bible studies at Nancy's request.

Then, while jogging one evening, he found various Bible verses and the recent Bible study topic rolling around inside him. Kevin finally dropped to his knees in some fresh-cut hay a mile or two down that country road and prayed simply, "I don't know about all of this, but I know that this Jesus is what it's all about."

## THE NEXT CHAPTER

SHORTLY THEREAFTER, the newly converted couple hastily married and began blending their family (she brought one child and he brought two from a previous marriage) and integrating their faith into life. Sunday after Sunday I would see them sitting in the front row of our newly formed church. If the story ended there, our team could thank God again for His healing touch. But we led Kevin to yet another important door.

He had soured on police work and left the force shortly after solving his partner's murder. When I found that he needed a job, I hired him as a restaurant shift supervisor at the truck stop I owned with my partner, Ted Crew. This gave Kevin steady employment and gave me a chance to continue discipling him in his newfound faith. Had I not been "doing" life and faith in a team context, I would never have met Nancy or Kevin, and all of us would have been the poorer for it in more ways than one.

Today Nancy works with computers, and Kevin has been police chief at Connecticut's Windsor Police Department since 1987. In the twenty-one years since Christ used our team to reach them with His truth and encourage them in their walk of faith, this couple has both hosted and led home Bible studies and taken many divine appointments with unbelieving friends, family, neighbors, coworkers, and strangers.

Wouldn't it be great if every town had a committed believer serving as its chief of police? Kevin not only treats his staff with Christian love, he also holds small-group Bible studies in his office. At one time, he would never have darkened the door of a church or imagined himself becoming a Christian. But he eventually felt comfortable investigating God because our team provided a safe, less formal environment.

The Searles value networks of faith because they personally so richly benefited from them. But anyone interested in recognizing and keeping divine appointments does well to equip themselves likewise.

## TEAM PERKS

AT THIS point, you may be wondering what team building has to do with divine appointments. Don't most divine appointments take place in serendipitous, one-on-one situations? Yes. Still, with the support of a handpicked group of believers, you have a human resources department with personality and passion at your disposal. For instance, you can quickly access help on how to sensitively field tough questions like Nancy's. By definition, a team is a wealthy bank of collective biblical knowledge and often hard-won wisdom. Regularly drawing on that bank can also put the uncertainties associated with divine appointments into proper perspective.

Building a spiritual team is like building a baseball team. With baseball, you don't want all catchers or all pitchers. You must have balance to win. The same with your spiritual team. You want people with different spiritual gifts. For example, if you are going to start an evangelistic home Bible study, you will have the best chance at success if you have a team of people with these gifts: hospitality, mercy, teaching, evangelism, and faith. If I were building this team, I would have as its cornerstone someone with the gift of faith. That person knows by faith that this venture will work, and he will be praying people into the kingdom. Without hospitality, people won't relax. Without mercy, people who have deep hurts or needs won't be cared for. Without good teaching, they won't get a clear picture of Christ and how He can meet their needs. Without the evangelist, who will bring closure?

In the most basic sense, a tight-knit team will help you stay ready, willing, and excited to be involved in God's plans. That's not always easy—especially solo—given the hurly-burly nature of twenty-first-century life. Maintaining personal integrity *and* fulfilling the Great Commission take no small amount of concentration. But when you seek to be way out there for Jesus on the mission God has given you, your team can keep you accountable.

"The average Christian never verbalizes to his fellow Christian, 'I am committed to reaching my neighbor.' They do it in isolation," says Joseph Aldrich, author of *Lifestyle Evangelism* and *Gentle Persuasion*. "But when we ask for prayer, then the guy is going to say, 'Well, you said you were praying about sharing with Sally or Bill. Did you?'"[1]

A team also doubles as a mini newsroom. God is out there with you in the mission field. A team gives you a place to report His activity—to celebrate kingdom progress and sound off about inevitable frustrations. This type of information loop will give you many fresh snapshots of the Lord at work in the gray zone, the places where the lives of believers and unbelievers overlap.

"If you're poor in faith, get around some people who are rich in faith," says Aldrich. "If you're poor in communicating the gospel, get around some people who are rich and listen because success leaves clues."[2]

## FAMILY TIES

SOMETIMES YOU won't need to look far. For instance, we formed another great team through our family ties. When our daughter, Beth, and her husband, Marvin, sense a divine appointment in the making, they call us. We call them when the tables turn. In either case, prayers begin when we put the phone receiver down. The circle of support enlarges when their three daughters—our precious little grandchildren—start praying too.

One of the more recent and memorable examples of our family's teamwork took place at my son-in-law's

Mobile gas station in Simsbury, Connecticut. Soft-spoken Michelle had worked there for eight months when Marvin sensed a divine appointment afoot. He guessed that she had some spiritual needs, but before speaking to her about them, he talked to Beth and to Betty and me. We prayed for this young woman and asked God to show us how we might be available.

When new people come into your life—be it the painter, the plumber, or the neighbor lady who comes over to look at the cat—you have to assume that God put them on your radar screen. That doesn't mean you will necessarily lead them to Christ. But again, you have to assume that nobody comes into your life by accident.

As Marvin started getting to know Michelle, he learned she had grown up in a broken home and had lived in several Midwestern states. At age sixteen, she had gotten pregnant and then lost the child by miscarriage. Before walking out of the room in disgust, the doctor had told her that she was too young to have a baby anyway.

Now twenty-four and the mother of a four-year-old daughter, Tessa—the product of another broken relationship—Michelle lived at home with her mother and stepfather and still struggled to make ends meet. She slept on a sofa in their sparsely furnished apartment. Yet she worked hard at the gas station, and Marvin quickly trusted her with a number of responsibilities.

## OPPORTUNITIES KNOCK

MICHELLE, IN turn, trusted Marvin from time to time with her thoughts and feelings, and their conversations eventually revealed her spiritual journey. One day Michelle shared that as an adolescent, she would sit in the center of her room and talk aloud. She figured she was borderline schizophrenic. However, looking back, she wonders if she wasn't just trying to pray in the midst of her loneliness.

Meanwhile, our team kept praying and listening to Marvin's regular reports on how Michelle was doing. He not only challenged her to accept Christ as her personal Savior, but he also gave her the little green booklet published by Campus Crusade for Christ called "Would You Like to Know God Personally?" She considered that idea for one week. All the while, strange dreams of darkness and light warred within her. Could a battle over her soul be taking place in her subconscious?

After seven days of living in this state of flux, she walked out into the middle of a big field on the outskirts of our little New England town and confessed everything "bad" that she had done. There in the quietness of that pastoral place, she accepted Christ and through Him rejected all her guilt and shame at last.

On her next shift she told Marvin about her conversion experience, and he promptly directed her to the women's Bible study Betty leads at our church on Friday mornings. There Michelle met a group of women who nurtured her in her faith. Weeks later, our team helped her move into a new apartment, gave her some furniture, and stocked her pantry.

## WAY OUT OF MY COMFORT ZONE

SHORTLY AFTER that moving day, Michelle got bad news. Her half-sister had overdosed on heroin and died. Would I speak at the funeral to give her family some hope? At first I resisted. "I don't do funerals!" I said to my team. "This is way out of my comfort zone. I don't know these people." Finally, under the influence of Betty, Beth, Marvin, and the Holy Spirit, I agreed. And so, I met Michelle's stepfather and other extended family. Furthermore, before closing the service, I explained how Christ loves each one, how it's possible to know God personally, and how the gap between Him and us has been bridged. Forty of the sixty people gathered prayed the sinner's prayer. This was a real God thing.

Two weeks later, after my team and I had prayed about it, I invited her stepfather to go out for coffee. I wanted to find out how he was coping with the death and to discuss the funeral. What did the tragedy mean to him? Several cups later, I led him to Christ by sharing how God alone can heal a broken heart.

Not all divine appointments lead to such immediate conversions. And when these miracles happen, the hard work of discipleship remains. But the point is that the blessing of all this spiritual sowing and reaping started when Marvin kept a divine appointment with Michelle and shared that news with us, his team. Without teamwork-based follow-up, who knows if she would have plugged into Betty's Bible study at church or met other believers who could help her reach out to her loved ones?

## BUILDING BUILDERS

THERE IS strength in numbers. In Luke 9, Jesus called His twelve disciples together and then sent them out. I consider this a prototypical evangelistic model. In Luke 10, He appointed seventy-two others and dispatched them in twos to visit towns.

Paul and Timothy make one of the greatest duos in the New Testament. In this mentoring relationship, Paul nurtured Timothy and equipped him to minister as his son in the faith. But Paul didn't stop with Timothy. He continued building teams wherever he went, and he encouraged Timothy to do likewise.

Like Paul, teammates ideally seek to build builders. In

this way, the kingdom of God spreads exponentially. So making yourself more available for divine appointments may mean joining a team and then forming a new one.

## THE RECONCILIATION ENDGAME

DO YOU still consider yourself more of a Lone Ranger? Think again. Even Jesus—God in the flesh—didn't minister alone. He pulled together a band of twelve to help Him get the Word out. The original disciples came from different backgrounds—everything from carpentry to fishing to tax collecting—and brought both strengths and weaknesses to that team. For instance, by recruiting the physician Luke, Jesus gained a detail-oriented teammate who wrote the most vivid gospel and recorded the early church's history in the book of Acts.

With their collective brains, brawn, and faith, Christ's first team of disciples ministered with extraordinary effectiveness to all sorts of people. Like them, you will get a stronger taste of God's reconciling power when you join with others to follow Him. After all, divine appointments ultimately point to the power of Christ's love to reconcile us to God. But God's brand of reconciliation serves to mend fences at every point of difference—between races, genders, socio-economic classes, ages, and so on.

This power seems unbelievable until you've experienced it. For instance, had someone told me when I first moved to New England that my two best friends and teammates would be a former Mafia drug runner and a senior vice president with a big Hartford-based insurance company, I would have considered them loopy. But when believers gather to reach out to people with whom they may share no natural affinity, the team itself is living proof of God's reconciling power.

Learning that God's love is greater than our differences doesn't always come easily—especially without the support of a Christ-centered team. Yet 2 Corinthians 5:17-20 encourages this kind of ministry: "Therefore, if anyone is in Christ, he is a new creation; the old has gone, the new has come! All this is from God, who reconciled us to himself through Christ and gave us the ministry of reconciliation. . . . We are therefore Christ's ambassadors, as though God were making his appeal through us."

That appeal involves not only presenting Christ's saving grace but also modeling the fruit of the Spirit—love, joy, peace, patience, kindness, goodness, faithfulness, gentleness, and self-control (Galatians 5:22-23). Teams nurture both.

## NUTS-N-BOLTS

DURING OUR thirty-five years of leading evangelistic home Bible studies and encouraging teamwork in reaching unbelievers with the claims of Christ, Betty and I have determined that the ideal team member shows

- total commitment to Jesus Christ,
- enthusiasm for Christ's Great Commission,
- optimism in God's faithfulness,
- reliance on the Holy Spirit,
- flexibility and resilience,
- motivation to get equipped for maximum availability,
- confidence in being able to contribute to the team,
- dedication to reaching out and seeing the team's mission through,
- a sense of humor and an upbeat, positive attitude,

- good listening skills,
- patience as God works in the team and the people with whom it has contact, and
- faith that the team is winsome.

Throughout this chapter, I've mostly mentioned teams with four or more members. However, Jesus said, "For where two or three come together in my name, there am I with them" (Matthew 18:20). You don't need to gather half your church to form an effective team. Finding just one person, a faithful partner, can make a fantastic team.

In terms of team building, Jesus models developing a core group and adds on from there. His insider team consisted of Peter, James, and John. I appreciate that model. My insider team, other than my wife, Betty, includes Bryan Marcoux and David Findley. Those characters are the two best friends and teammates I referred to earlier. Both have been invaluable inspirations, fellow believers I could trust to help me give my best availability to God. However, the most colorful teamwork illustration that stands out involves Bryan.

## TIME CRUNCHES

WHEN I consider the blessing of our two-man team, I remember how he helped me with a divine appointment that presented itself when I was frantically trying to open a second Dunkin' Donuts shop in Southington, Connecticut. The town zoning officer had at the last minute prohibited our opening due to a petty code issue. So with money in the register and employees waiting in uniform to work, I had to keep the doors locked on the grand-opening day while we moved toward resolution.

I knew I would face a "Closed" sign at the new shop for at least a week. So I began compulsively counting each day's lost revenue against each day's overhead. Anxiety frayed my nerves, drained my patience, and narrowed my focus to one thing—cutting the red tape that was choking our business. Winning the inspector's approval engrossed so much of my time and energy, it's a wonder I remembered to brush my teeth that week.

As I raced to get my coffee from the original donut shop next to my office, I noticed a middle-aged man slouched over one of the shop's patio tables in that morning's frosty first light. The day before, I had spotted him standing on the road. On both occasions, he half-heartedly held a cardboard sign that read, "WILL WORK FOR FOOD."

I viewed him and his sign as a curiosity at first because you don't see many homeless people in Southington, a bedroom community of mostly white-collar employees. I also felt a small surge of compassion, and compassion doesn't often register in my heart. I always say that Betty's got the gift of mercy, not me.

At the time, my business agenda seemed so much more pressing than his hunger. But there was no doubt I felt God grab me by the scruff of the neck to slow me down. Convicted by the Holy Spirit, I soon strolled over to the table outside. With every step I silently fretted that I had no time for a divine appointment.

"Hi, I'm Bob," I said, extending my hand. We shook, and I noted how cold, wooden, and grimy his grip felt. Dirt had accumulated under his fingernails, and his matted blond beard showed some crusty soup stains.

"Eh," he grunted. "The name's Jerry." Because the mercury had plunged past freezing the night before, I next asked him where he had slept. Apparently, he had bedded down under the interstate bridge and hadn't yet rustled up any breakfast.

I thought about his dirty hands and his badly chapped lips as I whipped together a huge breakfast sandwich at our Dunkin' Donuts shop. As I poured Jerry's orange juice and coffee into large Styrofoam cups, I reflected on the irony of his outfit. He wore a hodgepodge of dated clothing coupled with oversized black patent leather shoes—the high-gloss kind you wear to weddings—and no socks. That's when it hit me. This was a divine appointment. Jesus Christ was serving the needy through a reluctant, yet yielding, Bob Jacks.

# TEAM 911

ALTHOUGH I occasionally spoke at a Sunday Breakfast Mission when we lived in Wilmington, Delaware, I never really considered myself called to minister to street people like Jerry. It seemed too tall an order. But that morning, the Holy Spirit put me in his shoes, and my hesitation to get involved became a non-issue.

"Who can I call? What can I do for Jerry? Dear Lord, help this man," I feverishly prayed during the brisk walk back to my office. "Dear Lord, help me!"

Plopping into my chair, I hunched forward over my desk still strewn with unfinished business. Despite that perplexing distraction, I tried to assemble my thoughts and somehow resisted the temptation to lock my door and avoid the whole thing.

Then it dawned on me that I wasn't trying to avoid Jerry. I was running from myself. It's so human to try to protect yourself from your own personal pain, much less someone else's. But I knew God put that man in my path for a reason. I believe He always does.

Later, as we sipped coffee together on the Dunkin' Donuts patio, Jerry shared his story. He hailed from Portland, Oregon—three thousand miles away. One evening, several months earlier, he and his wife left their six-month-old baby with his mother-in-law so they could go out for dinner and a movie. During their date, the baby died of Sudden Infant Death Syndrome (SIDS). The tragedy shook him badly, and he ran from the trouble at home. He left his wife and a successful landscaping business.

I asked Jerry if he had a broken heart, but I didn't need to pose this question. Tears streamed down his grimy face, and he whispered, "Yes." When I asked him if he knew Who could heal him, he snuffled and said "yes" again. Just a week earlier, he had prayed to receive Christ at a local mission in Massachusetts. Now he wanted to clean up and return to Portland to reconcile with his family.

So I let my fingers do the walking to my team. Betty prayed with me about Jerry on the telephone first. Then I rang Bryan and expected him to tie on a red cape and fly to the rescue. Crestfallen hardly explains how I felt when he started coughing and listing all the reasons why he couldn't drop everything that second.

Yet fifteen minutes later, Bryan showed up and we went to work, first by purchasing Jerry a one-way bus ticket home. However, before putting him on the Greyhound, Bryan took him to the Salvation Army for a shower, a meal, some clean duds, and better-fitting shoes. He scoured the shelter, but in the end could not find a size 9D shoe for Jerry—until he spotted his own feet. Chuckling, Bryan bent down and started unlacing.

## Fresh Eyes

YOUR TEAMMATES, like my teammates, will never be perfect. They may balk at your plans or beef about your predicaments. Still, you've got to know that, in a pinch, they've got a heart like Bryan's—one big enough to make room for the most inconvenient opportunity to share God's love in word or deed.

But what about seemingly inconsequential divine appointments? Any passerby could deduce from Jerry's appearance that he had some unmet needs, that something had knocked his world off-kilter. Yet plenty of folks fall through the cracks because they seem so, well, ordinary. They don't inspire compassion at first glance and therefore you may not go the extra mile. However, when you can't see this reality, perhaps one of your teammates can.

C. S. Lewis eloquently addresses this deception of ordinariness:

> It is a serious thing to live in a society of possible
> gods and goddesses, to remember that the dullest
> and most uninteresting person you talk to may
> one day be a creature which if you saw it now,
> you would be strongly tempted to worship or
> else a horror and corruption such as you now
> meet, if at all, only in a nightmare. . . . There are
> no *ordinary* people. You have never met a mere
> mortal. . . . But it is immortals whom we joke
> with, work with, marry, snub and exploit—
> immortal horrors or everlasting splendours.
> . . . Next to the Blessed Sacrament itself, your
> neighbor is the holiest object presented to your
> senses.[3]

# KEEPING
## APPOINTMENTS

1. Kevin Searles' father told him to forget about God. Are there people in your world who have written God off? Why?

2. If Bob had discussed the sin of premarital sex with Nancy and Kevin when they began attending the Bible study, where might they be today?

3. Is it appropriate to discuss moral issues with unbelievers? Why or why not?

4. When Bob spoke at the funeral, forty of the sixty people in attendance accepted Christ. Bob has no idea how to follow up. Should he give invitations when he cannot follow up with discipleship? Why or why not?

5. As you consider the nuts-n-bolts of the ideal team member, how do you stack up?

6. If you decided to build a team, whom would you recruit and why?

7. Why are teams often more effective than Lone Rangers in reaching unbelievers?

8. Do busy, time-starved people have a valid reason to postpone stepping out of their comfort zone when God is nudging them toward a divine appointment?

9. Name some of the reasons unbelievers might begin searching for spiritual answers.

10. What questions do unbelievers often have regarding the institutional church?

11. Why do many unbelievers balk at going to a Sunday-morning church service?

12. How do you know when it's time to witness to someone in your world?

13. What are the risks involved in sharing your testimony with an unbeliever?

# PLATFORMS FOR MINISTRY

BY BOB JACKS

*One of the most amazing revelations of God comes when we learn that it is in the most commonplace things that the Deity of Jesus Christ is realized.*

—OSWALD CHAMBERS, *MY UTMOST FOR HIS HIGHEST*, FEBRUARY 7

*I am obligated both to Greeks and non-Greeks, both to the wise and the foolish. That is why I am so eager to preach the gospel also to you who are at Rome.*

—ROMANS 1:14-15

∿    ∿    ∿

GARY EARL CLAIMS THAT what works in football works in business: keep moving your legs, and you'll get ahead of the game. That philosophy prompted the blond boy-wonder to scramble up the career ladder without much noticeable slippage. Then his wife, Pat, popped his bubble with the sharpest pin, and the freefall started. Not only did she not love him—she didn't *like* him either. Money in the bank didn't matter two cents to her and, as it turns out, neither did their roomy home nestled in the rolling hills of upscale Granby, Connecticut.

Looking back to that fall day in 1995, the energetic Gary says the news stupefied him. How could he sell with the Midas touch and not notice his marriage tarnishing? He took a deep breath and braced himself as Pat informed him of her plans. To his surprise, instead of plunking down an ultimatum or packing her bags and moving out with their five children, she joylessly promised to honor her marriage vows.

The first tidal wave of news, that he was unloved and disliked, nearly drowned him in anguish. It didn't help that Pat—his even-tempered, put-together wife—dug her heels in only because she believed divorce didn't fly with God. Though clueless about the depth of her discontent, he had sensed her Christian conviction growing since 1992. That's when she'd recommitted her life at Betty's Bible study after a workout buddy at the gym invited her to attend. As usual, I began "husband duty"—praying for Gary, that by divine appointment he too would come to faith in Christ.

Instead, Gary briefly imagined that his savvy business acumen would help him negotiate his troubling marital matters. When those attempts proved worthless, he reacted like so many living in a thorny love nest. He aimlessly flew through the next few months feeling socked in by an emotional fog that he couldn't lift. In the meantime, he continued attending church—Gary considered himself religious. But he had never viewed God as a lighthouse in such pea-soup conditions. Once he joined Pat for a potluck Bible study at our house, but nothing came of it.

Still, life goes on, and friends threw a surprise thirty-sixth birthday party for Gary at the local pub a few weeks later. That's when he met my son-in-law a second time, the first time being when Pat introduced them at our potluck. The men mingled around the pool table and as beer after beer went bottoms up, Gary meandered over to greet Marvin. He recognized the handsome, quiet Southerner sipping Coca Cola. However, he frankly wondered if Marvin was crashing the beer party as an antagonistic Bible thumper. Soon Gary learned that a mutual friend had invited Marvin and with that settled, the two struck up a conversation that eventually touched on what was bugging the birthday boy.

## STARTING WITH SUDS

YOU MAY or may not agree that a divine appointment can take place over a beer—much less one sipped amid the smoke of the local bar. But that's exactly what happened between Gary and Marvin. As a result, Gary decided to accept Marvin's invitation to join him at a 6 A.M. men's Bible study the next day.

Gary operates like the Energizer Bunny, so the early hour didn't faze him a bit that January in 1996. But when he showed up, he realized too late that each man brought his own Bible—a book he didn't own. So after the group disbanded, Gary beelined for the nearby Christian bookstore. He laughs when he remembers whipping out his wallet and asking the clerk to pull a Bible for him. Before hopping to it, she wanted to know what *kind* of Bible he had in mind.

"What . . . uh . . . what do you mean?" Gary stammered with slight exasperation. "I want a 'Holy' Bible." The clerk quickly grasped Gary's seeker status and seized her opportunity by leading him to a towering wall of translations. Before leaving him to peruse, she suggested he open to John (the classic starting point for unbelievers) to compare each translation's readability.

Once Gary had resigned himself to the fact that this wouldn't be a five-minute shopping trip, he parked on the aisle stool. There he read John—and much of the New Testament—before walking out late afternoon with a study Bible tucked under his arm. Within that month, he accepted Christ.

"But I kept saying the sinner's prayer for a year just in case God was busy working on Clinton or somebody else," Gary says with a toothy smile under twinkling blue eyes.

## FORMAL VERSUS INFORMAL PLATFORMS

AS YOU ponder the possibility of divine appointments, remember the key ingredients. I've covered the importance of giving God 24/7 availability, viewing others with Christ's compassion, and teaming up with like-minded believers for prayer support and networking. Now it's time to address the various platforms on which all of these factors work together to minister in a world where people are crashing and bleeding on the highway of life.

Two types of platforms exist: formal and informal. A church service is an example of a formal platform. Yet this chapter focuses on informal platforms like the pub and the men's home Bible study Marvin used to reach Gary. Why? As it was in the first century, it is today. Jesus didn't hole up behind stained glass. He ministered primarily in public spots and in the dining and living rooms of ordinary people instead. He also ministered on boats—and remember that Paul ministered in prison cells. Like them, you need to meet unbelievers on their turf—where they live, work, and play—instead of expecting them to immediately join you at a formal platform like a Sunday-morning church service.

In the mid-1990s my daughter, Beth, and her husband, Marvin, began regularly entertaining international students enrolled at nearby Hartford University. Typically, they serve a home-cooked meal and give the students an opportunity to practice English and learn more about American culture.

Thanks to this informal platform, most of the students eventually join a home Bible study and find Christ. One Chinese couple stands out. Chang He worked as an Otis Elevator executive in China and arrived to earn a master's degree at Hartford. Her husband, Robert, joined her, having a desire to learn English and the American customs.

One night, after they had attended a home Bible study for about six months, Betty and I invited them to celebrate Chang He's birthday at our home with Beth and Marvin. I had been speaking to both Chang He and Robert about Christ. To my amazement, Robert said, "Ah, *Jesus* is the bridge to God." His wife, on the other hand, wasn't sure what God would do with her if she accepted Christ. Yet each took a leap of faith that night and prayed to receive Him. When Chang He blew out her birthday candles, Robert simply said, "Hmmm . . . two birthdays today."

With the exception of one woman from Taiwan, these students have all hailed from mainland China. How ironic is it that we have more of a platform with them here, informally, than we would there, formally. Of the five international students Beth and Marvin have "adopted," four have come to faith in Christ.

Our pastor, Dr. Jay Abramson, appreciates the very different roles formal and informal platforms serve. For instance, formal platforms usually pop up on church property as equipping hubs of discipleship, fellowship, and worship. Informal platforms, on the other hand, provide evangelism *satellites*. They include any place or activity outside church life that allows contact with unbelievers, however shallow.

When my partner and I built our first Dunkin' Donuts store, it came equipped with a full bakery to mix, proof, fry, and bake the entire product line for the store. Later, we built our first satellite and supplied that store with finished products produced at the main store. Then we built another and another until we had four Dunkin' Donuts satellites with all the products, signage, uniforms, and other attributes of the main store.

This is my concept of what an authentic church in the twenty-first century should be like. It is an equipping center from which members set up satellites in their homes, offices, schools, or workplaces. Examples of parachurch groups that support these satellites are Moms in Touch, Child Evangelism clubs, Lighthouses of Prayer, Youth for Christ, Young Life clubs, Lighthouse Bible studies, and Prison Fellowship. There is a wealth of information and help from groups like these to aid you in starting and maintaining a ministry. Ideally, these satellites make springboards to the formal church platforms. You may even want to develop your own satellite ministry. That's how most or all of the above started.

Here are a few informal platforms you might want to reconsider:

- Golf courses
- Tennis courts
- Swimming pools
- Field sports
- Health clubs
- Children's play groups
- Quilting clubs
- Hospitals
- Mom's groups
- Coffee klatches
- PTA meetings
- Neighborhood functions
- Newcomers clubs
- Dormitory rooms
- Foreign student groups
- Office settings
- Bridge clubs
- The workplace
- Pick-up basketball games
- Assisted-living facilities
- Nursing homes

## CULTURE SHOCK

THESE INFORMAL platforms provide nonthreatening, shallow entry points. Remember that the Holy Spirit may arrange plenty of divine appointments at these venues before calling the unbeliever to more formal involvement. Why? Because this type of gradual exposure lets the seeker explore who Christ is, what He accomplished, and how He can be real in his or her life—without experiencing church culture shock. It gives him or her a safe place to ask "dumb questions."

After all, believers and unbelievers can see formal platforms through very different glasses. For instance, churchgoers typically consider the ushers stationed at the doors on Sunday mornings as friendly folks. They're the people who shake hands, distribute bulletins, and gently hold the elbows of older ladies while they carefully slip into a pew. Ushers place poinsettias and Easter lilies on the windowsills during the high holidays and collect the weekly offerings. If the fire alarms go off, they direct traffic and exit the building last.

But Pastor Jay reminds that to the unchurched unbeliever, these very same men and women may seem less like "good cops" and more like a militia unit supervising an hour-long lockdown. Add an unfamiliar liturgy, especially if it's aerobic—lots of standing up, sitting down, and in some services, clapping hands—and the traditional church platform starts feeling like a foreign country, not a home.

No wonder the Bible is replete with stories of Jesus, the mastermind behind every divine appointment, who stepped onto informal platforms as He ministered. For instance, He met the woman at the well where she drew water every day at high noon (John 4:4-30). He dined with Mary and Martha in their home (Luke 10:38-42) and called Zacchaeus down from the sycamore-fig tree (Luke 19:1-9). He walked among tombs to encounter the possessed man who lived there (Mark 5:1-20). He dined with "sinners" at Matthew's home (Mark 2:15).

# THE NEED FACTOR

ULTIMATELY, NONE of these informal platforms is any more or less than what it sounds like. Each simply offers a stage upon which to rub shoulders with the lost. And those people are as unique as snowflakes, even if they blanket the same area. So if you study Jesus' ministry, you'll note that about half of His platform involved finding common ground. The other half involved perceiving needs and asking questions. Both worked as entrées into an unbeliever's world. Our challenge is to go and do likewise as the Holy Spirit provides discernment.

To determine the need factor, listen carefully. What information does that person share with you? What can you read between the lines? Paul offers some fundamental sensitivity training in Romans 12:9-13: "Love must be sincere. Hate what is evil; cling to what is good. Be devoted to one another in brotherly love. Honor one another above yourselves. Never be lacking in zeal, but keep your spiritual fervor, serving the Lord. Be joyful in hope, patient in affliction, faithful in prayer. Share with God's people who are in need. Practice hospitality."

When Jesus met the Samaritan woman at the well, a quintessential informal platform, He perceived her broken heart. Then He gently questioned her about her past. Being God, He could of course gather her whole story in a heartbeat. None possess Christ's clairvoyance, but when you follow His leading, you too will begin perceiving needs with more awareness.

"[Jesus] found the point of need in the individual's life, and then He shared the Good News," writes author Joseph Aldrich. "Part of the advantage of a relationship is that you can find that point of need in a person's life in which the gospel becomes good news. If the marriage is falling apart, you've got good news. If the person's financial world is falling apart, you've got good news. You don't approach two people in the same way."[1]

We recently had a new couple move into our neighborhood. Beth and Betty found out she was pregnant with twins and was having problems carrying them to maturity. They began to carry in meals, and we began to pray for her. She had a need; they addressed it.

## GOOD NEWS FOR BAD NEWS

GARY AND Pat—the couple I mentioned at the beginning of this chapter—found themselves in a crumbling relationship. With their broken hearts, they needed something beyond what they could buy to heal their marriage. To reach Gary, my son-in-law and his teammate James recognized the birthday party at the bar as an informal platform. They made themselves totally available to the Holy Spirit and, sure enough, the conversation with Gary slowly turned from sports and weather to something more. They talked about Gary's most pressing need and then quite naturally discussed the relevance of Christian faith on marriage matters.

Through this divine appointment, Marvin discovered the kind of openness in Gary that made it seem appropriate to refer him to another informal platform—the men's Bible study held weekly at 6 A.M. on a friend's winterized back porch. Regularly attending that spiritual support group helped Gary grow and begin to take better advantage of the discipleship available at church, the formal platform.

Months before, Paige, one of the women in Betty's Bible study, had considered the health club an informal platform. She met Pat there while cycling in the same row of stationary bikes. After getting acquainted in this casual setting, Paige invited Pat to the annual Christmas brunch at our house.

From Bible studies to Christmas brunches, we regularly use our home as a platform. Just after purchasing the old colonial, we contacted local architect Richard Schoenhardt to help us tastefully design an addition. Our goal involved comfortably seating up to seventy people in a family-room setting for outreach events.

When I share this construction project with others, they seem shocked. Then I remind them that traditional missionaries often sell all they own to head for a foreign mission field. Our zip code is our mission field, so this use of money and space isn't such a bad idea. Two families in Michigan (Ron and Terri Nicklaus, and Bart and Liz Bowser) recently built additions based on our model.

In any event, like the health club, the Christmas brunch represents an informal platform. Women gather to tour our historic home with its vintage decorations, to nibble on holiday goodies, and to reflect on the Christmas story. Betty always arranges for someone to share a testimony as well. After the brunch, Paige asked Pat if she'd like to check out Betty's Bible study. Pat agreed, and eventually she and Gary slid into their pew more spiritually hungry than ever before in their lives.

## WHY CHICAGO?

WHEN I have made myself available, sensed the presence of the Holy Spirit, and listened to my perceptions of someone's need, God has provided the most unlikely informal platforms for divine appointments. For instance, I recently hopped a shuttle bus from O'Hare Airport in Chicago to my hotel in a western suburb where I had a speaking engagement lined up at Wheaton College.

Upon landing, I called the hotel's 800 number and the pleasant lady on the line instructed me to stand on the round concrete island outside gate 3D. Van number 335 would pick me up in twelve minutes. Twenty minutes later, I started feeling a little anxious. If there's one thing I'm particular about, it's punctuality. However, an alpine-white van with bold green lettering wheeled up shortly.

As I carted my luggage to the curb, I expected the driver to stuff it into a tightly packed back section while I squeezed in. That's how it usually works. But that day, I had my pick of seats, so I got comfortable on the bench behind Robert, the driver. When the two-way radio crackled up front, I heard him tell the dispatcher that the five other passengers scheduled for pickup were no-shows.

Ten minutes later, Robert pulled into traffic with just me in tow. As the van sped up and merged onto the expressway, he casually asked what brought me to Chicago. I love this question! It gives me a wide-open door to witness. I told him I flew in to present a seminar at Wheaton College.

"What kind of seminar?" he asked, flipping the left turn signal off.

I explained that the seminar would give a group of denominational pastors ideas on how to lead a home Bible study for people who had for whatever reason tuned God out of their lives. I added that people who show up at these home Bible studies have often had a bad experience with the church, yet they're still curious about God—who He is, what He's like, and how He can be real in their lives.

## PLATFORM ON WHEELS

ROBERT SEEMED open to this kind of conversation, so I asked him if I could leave the bench seat behind him for the front bucket seat beside him. After climbing over the

106

console and strapping myself in, our discussion continued as we flew down the four-lane highway at seventy miles per hour. At this point, I sensed that the quiet van was a "God thing," an unlikely platform on wheels, empty but for one passenger—Jesus Christ in the person of Bob Jacks.

We serve an extreme God, one who operates on the edge if we are willing to follow Him there. So whenever these types of unlikely platforms slide underneath me, I can't help but remember the reason God put Christ on our platform, Earth. Luke 19:10 states it clearly: "For the Son of Man came to seek and to save what was lost."

From this Scripture, I conclude that if Christ lives in me and I call Him Lord, then He will use my life to accomplish His purpose. Still, many Christians have never sown or reaped in God's great mission field. Maybe it's because they don't recognize the Roberts in this world—the needy people the Lord puts you eyeball-to-eyeball with on a platform you'd never be able to build.

As we clipped along, I asked Robert about his life. First he told me about his eight-year-old daughter from his first marriage who lives in another state and his three-month-old daughter from his recent second marriage. Then he explained why he started moonlighting behind the shuttle bus wheel. The small commuter airline that employed him as a pilot had suffered financial setbacks recently, and that forced him to make ends meet with a second job. He sighed and admitted that the packed schedule stressed his family life.

Do you see the need? After we cleared the tollbooth, I learned more. Robert matter-of-factly explained that he wrote off church long ago because of all the impossible "do's and don'ts." If it took good works to get to heaven, he figured he was a goner. Still, this man prayed the Lord's Prayer nightly and would often think of his needs during the recitation.

# THE MESSAGE

BECAUSE OF distorted teaching or an unpleasant brush with the church, people like Robert—people who sense an empty God-shaped place in their heart—create their own "safe" spiritual quest apart from a formal platform. Though outside of the church, they're open to interacting with God in a way that meets their deepest needs.

As we pulled under the hotel awning, I felt the Holy Spirit prompting me to share the booklet "Would You Like to Know God Personally?" I carry with me everywhere. Several excuses popped into my head. For one, we were parked in a traffic circle with our hazard lights blinking. Two, I didn't know exactly where the booklet was in the four compartments of my briefcase. Have you ever had those kinds of debates with the Lord?

"Do you mind if I share this little green booklet?" I finally asked while fumbling with my briefcase clips and zippers. "It might help you on your spiritual journey." Robert didn't mind, and in a matter of minutes he prayed the sinner's prayer with me. Incidentally, he later mailed a thank-you note. The point is, perhaps hundreds of other Christian passengers had wondered about their shuttle driver's spiritual life. But without addressing his needs with Christ's love, they never got this kind of response.

# OTHER STEPPING-STONES

DIVINE APPOINTMENTS can take place anywhere at any time. Planes, trains, and automobiles—you name it. For you, it might involve photography, cooking, cars, surfing, computers, or kids. Platform possibilities seem endless. I find that my business background makes one of the surest stepping-stones to sharing my faith.

For instance, when Ted Crew and I owned a truck stop, we had a full-time chaplain (Glen Hilt), who conducted services and provided Christian counseling in an untraditional chapel—a permanently parked semi-truck trailer. It seated up to twenty-five truckers, and every year between fifty to eighty men and women found the Lord there, while countless others rededicated their lives to Christ. Most churches would die for this many converts.

My business platform has taken on many different forms. Another shaped up when I managed a group of research engineers at DuPont's world headquarters in Wilmington, Delaware. Before making a total commitment to Christ, I had been reading Keith Miller's book, *A Taste of New Wine*. In it, he described how he started a Bible study at a major oil company's headquarters.

When I looked around my workplace, I saw a high-tech staff with degrees from M.I.T. and Stanford. Could I "come out" with my faith to these hardcore scientific types? No way! Yet when I gave God 100 percent availability—my total commitment—divine appointments immediately appeared.

## OPEN DOORS AT DUPONT

THE DOORS at DuPont first opened when a Research Fellow entered my office one morning and gently closed the door. He wanted me to speak to a close friend and former coworker at headquarters who lay dying of terminal cancer. What? How did this guy even know that I was a Christian?

I agreed and asked him to pray with me before we visited her in the hospital over our lunch hour. Before bowing, I rang the only other believer I knew on the premises. Sam Workman had accepted Christ at one of our home

Bible studies, and I knew I could count on him to join us in prayer.

As our wingtips clicked on the hospital's linoleum floors, I wondered what I could possibly say. I didn't know this lady and barely knew Dick, the man who had dropped in hours earlier. When he introduced me to Kathy, the cancer patient, she spoke first.

"Thank God you're here," she whispered.

"That's why we're here," I replied without hesitation. "To talk with you about God."

It turns out that she'd given her life to Christ the night before after watching a telecast Billy Graham crusade. But she didn't fully understand what the decision meant. As she lay on her deathbed, God provided a divine appointment for me to give her the assurance of salvation.

Back at the office, Dick was so excited that the Lord had answered our prayers that he suggested starting a Bible study. So we did, and all of sudden Christians came out of the woodwork to attend. I never guessed that our lab director believed in Christ, but when the study group grew bigger, we met in his office.

As a result of that one Bible study at DuPont's Engineering Research & Development Lab, a dozen or so started throughout the company headquarters. Little is much when God is in it!

## Pasta Shop Possibilities

MY BUSINESS platform also partially explains why Kristy Slayton, a woman who attended Betty's Bible study, introduced me to Kim and Scott Morrison, her stepdaughter and son-in-law. Kristy knew my success in being co-owner of Dunkin' Donuts shops in the area, and she figured I might be able to give them some hearty business advice along with a taste of the gospel.

I learned more about Kim and Scott after I met Moe Slayton—Kristy's husband and Kim's father—for coffee at a bagel shop. Though now retired, at the time he served as the chairman of a major Hartford-based investment firm. For us, business made a bridge. Moe knew I had succeeded in various retail food endeavors, and as we strategized, Scott unexpectedly popped in the shop.

"Hey, Scott!" Moe called. "Come over. I want you to meet someone." Before Scott headed back to their pasta shop with his breakfast, he and I arranged to meet along with Kim bright and early on Saturday to review their business plan.

The Morrisons had excitedly opened their shop in Avon a couple of years prior, but it began taking the bounce out of their steps as it dipped deeper into the red. Thus far, nothing had helped the situation—even as they worked sixteen-hour days trying to hold financial ground. So while the sauces simmered and the water boiled, I sat with them doodling numbers on a napkin. We gradually rewrote their business plan and included a new location, which helped them turn the financial tide.

In the meantime, while talking about margins and marketing, I learned more about the two biggest needs in the Morrisons' life—stability for their fledgling business and better health for their toddler daughter, Megan. Betty and I had been praying for this little girl long before we met her or her parents. She was born with Down's syndrome, a heart defect, and a condition that prevented her from breathing normally.

## BREAKTHROUGHS

ON THE drive to the pasta shop for our follow-up meeting, I sensed God telling me that it was time to share my faith with the Morrisons. Would they consider me silly for pulling out my worn little green booklet? Again I heard that "voice in my head"—the way my granddaughter Anna describes God's call. It said, "Now is the time."

After we finished our paperwork that morning, I asked them about their relationship with God. I told them I had been praying for them, and that I would like to share how they could know God personally. I held the little green booklet in my hand once again. Would that be okay?

"Yes," they said in unison.

I soon learned that these two had less than glowing faith flashbacks. Growing up in the church, they sang in the choir and attended parochial schools. But they classified church involvement as a duty. Plus, both had furtively questioned God as they peered at their disabled newborn lying jaundiced under the hospital's heat lamp.

"Why did You do this to us, God? We've been good people," Kim recalled thinking.

But between Megan and the business, they had needs they couldn't get met—no matter how they tried and cried. So while they answered ringing phones and served up to-go orders, I shared my faith in Jesus Christ. I explained that He could meet needs and provide peace on the deepest level.

When they accepted Jesus Christ, despite all the distractions, I referred them to a home Bible study for prayer support and more exposure to the gospel's relevance. When they recently took Megan to Cincinnati for a special surgery, I got two local Navigators—Kent and Jill Schellhouse—to pray for the family and visit them in the hospital.

## MIRACLE AT STARBUCKS

INCIDENTALLY, MOE Slayton and I met again months later when he was in town for the delivery of Kim's second child.

I had prayed for nearly five years that Moe would receive Christ. After making the appointment for coffee, Betty, Beth, and Marvin prayed for our meeting. Over coffee at Starbucks, I soon realized that this was the divine appointment that would be the turning point for Moe. He accepted Christ and within two weeks had shared his testimony with his church in Florida. These days, we are studying Bill Bright's *Five Steps of Christian Growth* together over the phone to help him on his spiritual journey.

## ACCOUNTABILITY BY THE NUMBERS

CAN YOU see how divine appointments develop when you invite the Holy Spirit to mix Christ, compassion, teams, and platforms to meet needs? The business platform has given me access to so many—from young entrepreneurs like the Morrisons to self-made millionaires. It seems that before these folks knew anything about Bob Jacks's faith in Christ, they viewed me as credible based on my success in business.

God can use that as a platform! And He has—through divine appointments with both unbelievers *and* believers. For instance, Paul Brewer's wife, Barb, cultivated his interest in Christ in the late 1980s. I met him a few years later at church. But I never really knew where he stood spiritually, or if he needed more accountability.

When I discovered that he worked in Hartford as a financial adviser, I recognized an opportunity to find out. I asked him to review some of my accounts and, perhaps, to manage some of that money. He later confessed that he felt intimidated by my spiritual zeal, but also intrigued by my business acumen. So he decided to give an accountability partnership a try.

Today, Paul and I meet at 7 A.M. most Wednesdays at a

cheery roadside café. Over a muffin and steaming coffee, we spend an hour discussing various entries in our leather-bound Oswald Chambers study book and journal, *My Utmost for His Highest*. I find that following this daily devotional book together works very well in discipling men.

Committing to an accountability relationship has amplified his faith outside of the church walls, making him more available for divine appointments. Specifically, he says he's got more of a "spiritual filter" on all aspects of his life.

Paul reports that this makes him feel and act less self-ishly—something people beyond his family have noticed. For instance, after a freak accident in which a hockey puck mortally wounded a high school player in the head, another parent hanging around the rink where Paul volunteers as a coach asked for his opinion. "The guy said, 'From God's standpoint, what do *you* make of it?'" Paul recalls. "That kind of comment gave me the sense that people are starting to come to me as a resource."

## LIGHTHOUSE BIBLE STUDIES

OTHER THAN business, Betty and I have used our home as our other primary platform for ministry. For the past thirty-five years, we have hosted seeker Bible studies there that are patterned after the Your Home a Lighthouse concept mentioned in chapter 2. These Bible studies make no substitute for church. Rather, like all informal platforms, they act as springboards to the church.

This platform has helped us introduce hundreds of unbelievers to the gospel in a nonthreatening setting—so much so that we eventually spread gravel over a section of our lawn for extra parking space. As I mentioned earlier, we also built a bigger family room with comfy couches and chairs to accommodate more people.

But you don't have to take out a home improvement loan to minister this way. You just need a team, a place, and some simple refreshments—or a potluck spaghetti dinner, as was the case at a recent study at Maria and Paul Selion's home. Like most of the other home Bible studies we've helped launch, this one starts at 6 P.M. on the second Wednesday night of every month.

As about twenty-five people mingled around the feast spread over their tile-topped kitchen island, all sorts of conversations sprouted about news, weather, jobs, and kids. (Don't feel you need twenty-five people for an evangelistic Bible study. Some of our most effective studies have started with two or three people.) The casual supper gave everyone a chance to unwind from the workday. At seven o'clock, people slowly progressed into the living room where Dave Findley—my friend, teammate, and Sunday school coteacher—sat looking like Johnny Cash, dressed head-to-toe in black.

But instead of diving into the short message he'd prepared from the book of Luke, Dave brought up the World Series to establish common ground. Then, to relate better to the group, he explained a little bit about what's happening in his life. If discouraged, he feels free to share that. Why? People can relate. Ultimately, like all platforms, this platform aims to meet needs with the gospel.

"Do you have something in your life that only God can solve?" Dave will eventually ask.

## MEET THE HOSTS

THE SELIONS started hosting a home Bible study about four years ago because their faith adventure began after attending one. Looking back, Maria remembers trying so hard to maintain what she calls a "Gone with the Wind" façade. Today she admits that it's easy to keep up that façade when life is good. But when their daughter was born with eye defects, when her father died of a massive heart attack, and when Paul's mother died three weeks later, this yuppie couple was left with unanswered questions and gaping spiritual needs.

Maria didn't even own a Bible at the time, but she and Paul sporadically attended church. One day, while skimming the church newsletter, a listing about home Bible studies piqued her interest. She almost skipped it, thinking there would be no child care. Yet rereading the newsletter told her otherwise. With no excuses, she showed up knowing at some level that her well-honed control-freak tendencies failed to pacify how lonely and desperate she felt inside.

Articulate and funny, Maria soon fit into the group. The dynamic couple eventually found the truth—that only Jesus satisfies—and as new Christians they opened their home to share that. But they're not on this platform alone.

## GUIDELINES FOR FIRST-TIMERS

AGAIN, TEAMWORK and platforms offer practical biblical ways to ready yourself for divine appointments. Jesus sent out His disciples to minister in twos. The apostle Paul always seemed to have a team, even when he was in prison. He ministered together with Luke, Barnabas, Silas, Timothy, and others.

A home Bible study leadership team can consist of couples, singles, or a combination of the two. They can divvy up the responsibilities of leading the Bible study, hosting the study by providing the home and the refreshments, and doing the invitations and follow-up. For this kind of meeting, we always invite two to three times more people than our home will accommodate.

Betty and I have worked so extensively off this platform that we have established simple guidelines to help first-timers make the widest comfort zone for unchurched persons. In this way, you can remove many barriers that might stand between them and Christ's message.

**Do:**

- Make people comfortable.
- Before the study, talk about things they are interested in—football, antiques, weather, their jobs.
- Take the phone off the hook or have someone nearby to answer it.
- Include people in conversation. Your leadership team should never all be in the same place at the same time.
- Be sensitive to timid or turned-off people. Include them in casual conversation before and after the study.
- Provide a paperback copy of a modern translation for each person there, the same copy you use yourself. You can direct them to a specific location by referring to page numbers first and then telling them where to look on the page. Many nonChristians are unable to locate books of the Bible. For example, you could say, "Tonight we'll start our study on page number 162 where we find chapter 10 of the book of John."
- Encourage people to take the Bible home.
- Be sensitive to time. Limit your Bible study to forty-five minutes or one hour, max.
- Cover all the material planned, even if you summarize.

∾ Prepare to love people rather than trying to force theology on them.

**Don't:**

∾ Pray, unless it is a sentence prayer for the refreshments.

∾ Play religious music.

∾ Talk about religion or your church.

∾ Be cliquish with your friends.

∾ Talk to others in a whisper.

∾ Berate, or even discuss, religious groups.

∾ Ask people to read aloud.

∾ Call on people by name, unless they have indicated they have a question or comment.

∾ Invite your pastor.

∾ Make it "churchy."

If you would like more practical information on how to penetrate your work world or neighborhood with the claims of Christ through Bible studies, read our book, *Your Home a Lighthouse* (NavPress, 1987).

# KEEPING
## APPOINTMENTS

1. How do you define your platform?

2. What are some platforms you might develop?

3. Going to church for an unbeliever may be like you going to _____.

4. What keeps you from sharing your faith? Would being with a team of like-minded believers help you reach out more? Why?

5. How long should a new believer "get ready" before sharing Christ's love with others?

6. Christ calls all believers to "go and make disciples." What is it to refuse that call?

7. Do you think a Your Home a Lighthouse Bible study would work in your world? In your neighborhood? Workplace? School? Social club? Other?

# CHAPTER SEVEN

# RELAXED ANTICIPATION

### BY BOB JACKS

*The people who influence us the most are not those who buttonhole us and talk to us, but those who live their lives like the stars in heaven and the lilies in the field, perfectly simply and unaffectedly. Those are the lives that mold us.*

—OSWALD CHAMBERS, *MY UTMOST FOR HIS HIGHEST,* MAY 18

*[Jesus prayed,] "I have given them the glory that you gave me, that they may be one as we are one: I in them and you in me. May they be brought to complete unity to let the world know that you sent me and have loved them even as you have loved me."*

—JOHN 17:22-23

෴     ෴     ෴

I DIDN'T CALL IT the cold shoulder at first. Instead I blamed my friend's emotional and physical distance on his busy schedule—or mine. I ran into him most often at church, and of late our exchanges had been uncharacteristically brief and punctuated with his nervous cough and averted eyes. So when he finally confronted me, I felt relieved. I wasn't losing my mind after all.

Tall and graying at the temples, my friend trained his light brown eyes on me for the first time in a month. How, he wondered aloud, could Bob Jacks have skipped church for a football game—especially on Communion Sunday? He didn't expect me to answer, because clearly he couldn't imagine one good reason for a fellow deacon (deacon chairman, nonetheless) like me to miss serving Communion. Flabbergasted by the irritation dripping off his words, I stood mute for a minute. Was that the problem, the real reason he had given me a frosty reception for weeks?

When I flashed back to the brisk fall day I played hooky, my then twelve-year-old son Michael appeared in my mind's eye racing from behind a two-story, green-shuttered, white house. He rolled out of bed at 5:30 A.M.,

Monday through Saturday, to toss the *Philadelphia Inquirer* from his bicycle around our Wilmington, Delaware, subdivision just thirty minutes outside of Philly. The paper route gave him fresh air and some spending money. But on Sundays, his list lengthened like Santa's on December 24th, and his papers got thick as medical textbooks. So to make the rounds in a timely way, we would load the papers into our station wagon.

One customer always left the payment for the last week's bill in a cup on his back porch. This payment equaled the cost of a dozen donuts to the penny. So before heading home to get ready for church, Michael and I would pick up a box to bring back to Betty and the other two children. But that day, the man came out back to pay him in person and offer three tickets to a Philadelphia Eagles football game that day as a thank-you for all the early-morning, rain-or-shine service.

## LET'S GO!

AS GUNG-HO a fan as they come, my boy probably had to scoop his jaw off the sidewalk. He rambled on about the team's quarterback, Sonny Jurgensen, with brotherly familiarity year 'round and had practically memorized the Eagles' playbook. However, until now Michael had to park himself in front of our black-and-white television to get in on the action. Landing a stadium seat and catching the live, full-color, fiery rivalry between the Eagles and the Washington Redskins looked like God's widest smile on him yet.

So when Michael breathlessly popped his head through the station wagon window, I immediately caught his exuberance and told him the plan sounded great. We double-timed it around the neighborhood to finish the route and rushed home to kidnap the unsuspecting eight-year-old

Beth. I phoned another deacon and asked him to cover for me. Then, after downing donuts and milk, the three of us bundled up and took off for Philadelphia's Franklin Field to enjoy our unexpected good fortune.

The score escapes me, but I still recall the excitement of watching a modern-day clash of giants as burly, green-shirted men ruthlessly pitted themselves against the hulks in red. And I'll never forget how that spectacle—along with the yelping hot-dog vendors, the flag-waving fans, the announcer's voice thundering over the crackling public address system—kept my kids spellbound.

When I snapped out of this reverie, the disgruntled deacon was waiting for an explanation with remarkably neutral body language. But he might as well have tightened his belt a couple of notches, cinched his necktie, crossed his arms, frowned, and started tapping his foot. He had become terribly uptight because in his mind I had violated a key point on his unwritten do's-and-don'ts list by passing up the Communion service for NFL entertainment.

## UNWRITTEN CODES

IF YOU'VE spent any time in Christian circles, you've probably stubbed your toe on somebody else's taboo. Though these unwritten approval codes vary from church to church, culture to culture, notorious no-no's include dancing, drinking, smoking, and playing cards. Add imperfect church attendance and *whoosh!* down the booby hatch you go! That explains how I fell from grace, according to him: I took my kids to a football game instead of to church.

In *The Grace Awakening,* Charles Swindoll confirms my suspicions—that believers seem particularly vulnerable to comparing each other. He speculates that because lifestyle differences make most Christians nervous, they develop unwritten codes that extend into minutia never addressed by the Word. Historically, these codes have handcuffed morality to such nonspiritual issues as how much bass can boom in music before it sounds too pagan, what kind of luxury car no good Christian should be caught dead driving, and why those who wear blue jeans to a Sunday-morning service offend God's fashion sense.

"The church is not a religious industry designed to turn out mass-produced reproductions on an assembly line. The Bible wasn't written to change us into cookie-cutter Christians or paper-doll saints," Swindoll writes of this conformity compulsion.

> On the contrary, the folks I read about in the Book are as different as Rahab and Esther, one a former prostitute and the other a queen . . . as unusual as Amos and Stephen, a fig-picker turned prophet and a deacon who became a martyr.
> . . . Before we will be able to demonstrate suffi-cient grace to let others be, we'll have to get rid of this legalistic tendency to compare.[1]

Given the way legalism divides the brethren, imagine the oil-and-water response it can create between believers and unbelievers! While Jesus never wore rose-colored glasses, He definitely extended grace that covered differ-ences of every description. His grace even covered flat-out sin. Yet how many of us embody His grace and relaxed anticipation when we face divine appointments?

## YOUR ANXIETY INDEX

DOES THE thought of a divine appointment give you but-terflies? I suspect that to view golden moments the way

Christ did, the average Joe or Jane believer needs to adopt a new modus operandi. To find out if you're uptight, take this quiz. Do you

- ∾ foster a judgmental, legalistic attitude toward yourself and others?
- ∾ worry about how someone's soul hangs in the balance between heaven and hell—and believe that it's up to you to tip the scales?
- ∾ fear rejection or mockery for celebrating Christ as the capital A answer?
- ∾ dread facing that blank, noncompute look from someone who considers the gospel as relevant in contemporary society as riding a quarter horse on the freeway?
- ∾ struggle to trust God with the outcomes of your divine appointments?

## LEGALISM DISMANTLED

IF YOU answered "yes" to one or all of these questions, you're in good company. Plenty of well-intentioned believers wrestle with the same fears and doubts. Even Jesus expressed a knowing sympathy when He said, "The spirit is willing, but the body is weak" (Matthew 26:41). He understands that you may be open to keeping a divine appointment, but hard-pressed to act when the opportunity mystically appears—be it around the coffee pot at work, on the bleachers at the Little League game, or under the hood of a neighbor's car.

To help you unwind, I have devoted the bulk of this chapter to dismantling the power of legalism—to throwing away the cookie cutter—because it is the most serious and most common killjoy to keeping divine appointments. After all, pinning yourself and others to the letter rather than the spirit of the law is like expecting to flawlessly complete a technically advanced obstacle course before landing at Christ's feet. This course demands that you bring willpower, practice, and a track record to prove that you are indeed *fit* for God's love. It's a pure do's-and-dont's exercise versus an acceptance of God's amazing grace.

"Many of us put God on Pier 40 as a niggling customs officer," writes Brennan Manning in *The Ragamuffin Gospel.* "He rifles through our moral suitcase to sort out our deeds, and then hands us a scorecard to tally up virtues and vices, so we can match baseball cards with Him on Judgment Day."[2]

But this is a biblically inaccurate picture. Rather, He's like the Daddy Warbucks of the cosmos. He dwells in a mansion and daily proves Himself winsome, powerful, generous, and tenderhearted toward all the little orphan Annies (and Andys) of the world. Compared to the kind of love you're used to, He may also seem daft—touched with a little amnesia. Manning illustrates this point with a simple story:

Four years ago in a large city in the far West, rumors spread that a certain Catholic woman was having visions of Jesus. The reports reached the archbishop. He decided to check her out. There is always a fine line between the authentic mystic and the lunatic fringe.

"Is it true, ma'am, that you have visions of Jesus?" asked the cleric.

"Yes," the woman replied simply.

"Well, the next time you have a vision, I want you to ask Jesus to tell you the sins that I confessed in my last confession."

The woman was stunned. "Did I hear you right, bishop? You actually want me to ask Jesus to tell me the sins of your past?"

"Exactly. Please call me if anything happens."

Ten days later, the woman notified her spiritual leader of a recent apparition. "Please come," she said.

Within the hour, the archbishop arrived. He trusted eye-to-eye contact. "You just told me on the telephone that you actually had a vision of Jesus. Did you do what I asked?"

"Yes, bishop, I asked Jesus to tell me the sins you confessed in your last confession."

The bishop leaned forward with anticipation. His eyes narrowed.

"What did Jesus say?"

She took his hand and gazed deep into his eyes. "Bishop," she said, "these are His exact words: I CAN'T REMEMBER."[3]

## GRACE FIRSTHAND

I'M CONVINCED works-based theology sabotages divine appointments in one way or another. After all, if *you* can't manage to conquer a moral obstacle course each day, why tell anybody else about the joy you've found in Christ? So caught up with navigating the many ins and outs, you may not really understand your own endgame—that it's receiving God's grace and knowing Jesus that count more than brownie points for "good" behavior. The grave problem is that without that no-strings-attached experience, you miss being an authentic Christian and, therefore, miss being an authentic witness.

Manning describes the fallout: "When the religious views of others interpose between us and the primary experience of Jesus as the Christ, we become unconvicted and unpersuasive travel agents handing out brochures to places we have never visited."[4] In other words, to show grace instead of judgment, you must humble yourself and accept what Manning calls the "handout of amazin' grace." Perhaps you loathe the thought of being on anyone's welfare roll—even the Lord's. But without a sure grip on that essential truth, you will never be the kind of compassionate, relaxed believer who takes divine appointments in God's stride.

Remember the ruffled feathers of my friend at church? He's entitled to his opinions. But be forewarned! Pointless and potentially hurtful conflict comes when you start imposing your list of do's and don'ts on others. When you reduce Christianity primarily to behavior modification, you have reduced your love for God to a performance-rated dog-and-pony show—religiosity versus spirituality.

You may memorize Scripture, tithe, regularly attend church, pray, support overseas missions, belong to committees, teach, preach, evangelize, and do, and do, and do. But if this kind of gold-star lapel pin compliance brings a whiff of pride, your witness will shrivel to phony, "can-do" drive in the eyes of the unbeliever. Furthermore, the degree of compliance you expect of yourself, you will be sorely tempted to uncompromisingly expect of others.

For instance, what if God were to call you to a divine appointment with someone like William (Billy) Coston? There's no way Billy would have made it past the morality cops without getting busted time and again. He spent twenty-four years hooked on drugs, alcohol, and pornography. Anyone with spiritual white gloves on wouldn't touch him—he must be someone else's divine appointment, right?

Well, it turns out that Billy didn't know the first thing about Jesus—except cursing with His name. So perhaps he would be given a little more leeway for not knowing any better. But when he found the Lord, God help him. Any lapse of judgment or stumble off the narrow path, and he might need to worry more about the flock accepting him back than the Shepherd.

## No Pretenses

HERE'S THE catch-22. Perhaps Billy's got what you lack— no pretenses about the hand that feeds him, no means to claim control over anyone, and no pride to lose in letting God be larger than life. After all, his troubles began early. At age two, the State of Connecticut deemed his home unfit for children and whisked him and his two brothers into foster care. When he realized that those folks were not his parents, like any other sensitive child, Billy obsessed about why his mom and dad would abandon him. He didn't know the full story—that they were alcoholics unable to properly parent. He only knew that he feared getting split up from his brothers, and that he missed being loved.

By age thirteen, he smoked cigarettes and pot. He guzzled beer. Then, at age fifteen, he graduated to harder stuff to quiet his confusion and numb his pain. He landed in jail at age eighteen for breaking into houses, and that's where he started snorting cocaine. The deeper he got into drugs and pornography, the emptier he felt. The correlation proved very direct. On this track, Billy eventually met a woman who worked the streets, and he had two children with her. They lived together, and he—not quite husband, not quite pimp—depended on her to bring money home while he ran drugs part time.

Looking back on those days, Billy says he honestly didn't know there was any other way to live. And he knew nothing about love because he had never received any. He felt stuck. He didn't want to go to hell, but he didn't know how to get to heaven. The word "saved" didn't ring any bells with him, but he knew it had something to do with religion. Billy needed a divine appointment.

The Holy Spirit scheduled it one night in 1991, when Billy sank to a lifetime low after violently clashing with his poker buddies. A fistfight broke out when they caught him cheating. In the midst of it, Billy smashed his girlfriend's face with a bag of pool balls.

When the dust settled, he surveyed the trashed apartment, the strung-out friends, the wide-eyed toddlers who had scurried for cover. He smelled danger and avarice in every room of his life. After so many years of the same, a bone weariness that comes from fighting a losing battle had crept into the deepest part of Billy. Running on the fumes of hope, he finally had hit "empty." To him, rolling to a stop meant suicide. He figured he'd go out on the town to buy one last fling before slipping away on an overdose of sleeping pills.

## SAVING POWER

THEN HIS friend and former drug-running buddy called. You guessed it—Bryan Marcoux. Perhaps the Holy Spirit called Bryan to call Billy because Bryan couldn't draw any lines in the sand. Much of what Billy was, Bryan had been. Bryan couldn't gallop up to Billy on his high horse and call down to him. He considered himself no better than anyone.

Do you honestly embrace that position as well?

Furthermore, in the absence of legalism, Billy could confess to Bryan and to God. This one-on-one connection with a nonjudgmental believer brought Billy to faith in Christ. Yet he suffered some serious setbacks along the way. He slipped back into abusing drugs a few times. Bryan persisted in discipling him, despite these disappointments. Eventually, he pushed Billy to check into David Wilkerson's rehab camp in Pennsylvania for an entire year. Not long after his release, Bryan put him on a bus headed to the treatment center for yet another year of therapy. After that second year, Billy beat his drug addiction for good and now works in maintenance at one of Wilkerson's halfway homes in New Jersey.

"It's just a blessing serving the Lord now, not the enemy," Billy reflects. His is the voice of humility, the voice that can speak something of God's grace into a divine appointment. He's someone who understands the saving power of the gospel with stark realism and immediacy.

Billy resonates with 2 Corinthians 12:9-10:

> But he said to me, "My grace is sufficient for you, for my power is made perfect in weakness." Therefore I will boast all the more gladly about my weaknesses, so that Christ's power may rest on me. That is why, for Christ's sake, I delight in weaknesses, in insults, in hardships, in persecutions, in difficulties. For when I am weak, then I am strong.

## NEW LIFE IN CHRIST

SOME FOLKS are wired in such a way that they can be religious about anything they put their mind to—eating fish three times a week; refusing to eat eggs but once a week; running Mondays, Wednesdays, and Fridays and resting Tuesdays, Thursdays, Saturdays, and Sundays; drinking eight glasses of water a day and not one drop of liquor.

But being a Christian is less about getting good at compliance—even to legitimate, God-breathed laws like the Ten Commandments—and more about getting good at letting Jesus Christ live His life through you. When you submit and give Him your total commitment, the ethereal outline of who He is mysteriously conforms to your exact measurements of life and limb. As the saying goes, we become "Jesus with skin on," albeit just a shadow of His graceful, loving presence.

This phenomenon reminds me of a story about a woefully average basketball player who consults with the genie in a bottle. She floats out and decides to grant his wish to play like NBA superstar Michael Jordan. In two winks, she has unzipped who he is and inserted all the talent and skill of the basketball star before zipping him back up again.

The next day happens to be a game day for the average Joe. When the coach finally calls him off the bench and puts him in, this guy is simply amazing. He's got game like he never had game. The cheerleaders drop their pompoms and stare with the crowd as he makes impossible three-point jump shots and steals from opponents who are all elbows. His newfound ability to play with power and grace surprises everyone.

Average Joe knows all along that he's not a natural. This ability was given to him. Truth be told, he partied the night before and had skipped plenty of practices. But when he let the powerhouse within call the shots, it tipped the court and helped him put a whole new spin on the ball.

The apostle John recorded Jesus as saying, "No one can come to me unless the Father who sent me draws him, and I will raise him up at the last day" (John 6:44). So as you step into a divine appointment, relax. It's not your responsibility to eloquently convince other people of their sin and need of Christ or to outplay them in the game of life. Besides, if you plow ahead and shoulder the work God intended for the Holy Spirit to do, you will undoubtedly put pressure on your relationships that could hinder—not help—others in finding Christ.

Ultimately, allowing the Holy Spirit to do His work liberates you to be yourself and strengthens your rapport with the unbeliever. God's busy, so you don't have to be. It's the Holy Spirit's job to hustle, not yours. It's that simple.

## THE "WHAT IFS"

IF YOU'VE still got the jitters, consider Linda Dillow's perspective. In *Calm My Anxious Heart,* she shares some of the ministry anxieties she faced while serving Christ with her husband, Jody, for more than twenty years in Europe and Asia. Political instability, sketchy housing arrangements, and ironclad cultural barriers to evangelism could have given her an ulcer and a headache every day she woke up on the mission field. But along the way, she learned to let go of that corporate, bottom-line mindset.

When she started worrying about all the "what ifs" associated with divine appointments—what if I would have quoted that Scripture, shared that personal revelation, showed up at that hour instead of this one—she meditated on Scripture. She found particular consolation in Jeremiah 17:5-8:

> This is what the LORD says: "Cursed is the one
> who trusts in man, who depends on flesh for his
> strength and whose heart turns away from the
> LORD. He will be like a bush in the wastelands;
> he will not see prosperity when it comes. He will
> dwell in the parched places of the desert, in a
> salt land where no one lives. But blessed is the

man who trusts in the LORD, whose confidence is in Him. He will be like a tree planted by the water that sends out its roots by the stream. It does not fear when heat comes; its leaves are always green. It has no worries in a year of drought and never fails to bear fruit."

During a three-year drought in her ministry, that Scripture watered her withered spirit and prompted her to pray it in her own words:

> Oh God, You know my tendency to try to control and help You out. I know that "helping You out" is what leads to an anxious heart. Forgive me. I don't want to trust in my own strength, in my strategies. I don't want to control or manipulate. Please, God, teach me what it means to not only trust You, but make You my total trust. I long to become that blessed woman whose roots are planted deep by Your river. As the heat of the trials increase, I long to trust instead of fear, to be content instead of anxious. Please keep my eyes focused on You so that my leaves will stay green and fruit will be produced in the midst of *What Ifs.*[5]

## NAIL BITING NOT NECESSARY

WHEN MY son Michael and I go bass fishing, we face plenty of "what ifs." I initially assumed that fishermen just threw out the worm—until I started fishing with him. But it's a sophisticated sport with plenty of variables, such as the type of bait, the water's depth, and seasonal feeding patterns. I recently learned that the time of day determines where the fish like to hang out, be it under rocks and lily pads or around the docks. He knows bass; he knows how they think.

Because my son's an enthusiast, he knows about these variables and owns a special bass fishing boat to fish as efficiently as possible. Meanwhile, I feel like biting my nails the second I step aboard. These fish are squirrelly. Even the thought of attempting to catch them unnerves me.

Nevertheless, my son models *relaxed anticipation* in the sport. And in this way, he always catches more fish than I do. Sure, his skills factor into the catch he pulls up. But I suspect that the biggest difference involves an attitudinal one. Michael remains alert without being uptight. The more relaxed he feels, the better he fishes.

Fishing for souls follows the same line, which allows me to be relaxed about reaching out to others with the claims of Christ. So in the spirit of my son's bass fishing composure and to lengthen my reach with the gospel, I recently started conversing with telemarketers who call our home. When they call, invariably during the dinner hour, I now respond by making a deal. I promise that I will give them two minutes to pitch their product if they will return the courtesy and give me two minutes.

If this doesn't require relaxed anticipation, I don't what does! Most people try to shorten, not lengthen, conversations with telemarketers. Yet I consider these callers divine appointments. So during my two-minute time slot, I ask them where they think they would spend eternity if they died that night. Can they think of a time when they prayed to receive Christ?

Reaching out in this way makes perfect sense to me. The call's on their nickel, so it's not my expense. It puts me in contact with people from different parts of the United States. Indeed, I believe it's an answer to my praying Jabez's prayer for God to expand my territory (see 1 Chronicles 4:10). And by approaching each call with relaxed anticipation, I have encouraged backsliders and prompted some unbelievers to reconsider accepting Christ. As a result, over the last year I have seen three tele-marketers come to faith in Christ, and others to reconsider where they are spiritually. But I have also changed tele-phone companies several times. As a matter of fact, I don't even know who my carrier is right now.

## ANGEL ENCOUNTER

STILL, WHEN you show someone the Way or pray for that person, it's easy to fret about the results. Will the message stick? Will he come to faith in Christ? Will God provide someone else to love and disciple her? The truth is, in some divine appointments, you'll never have the satisfaction of knowing anything about how the gospel took root in that person's life.

Matthew 13:1-9 relays Jesus' parable about the farmer who scattered seeds. As you may recall, because he sowed amply, seeds settled in a variety of places. Birds ate seeds that fell along the path. Other seeds landed on rocky ter-rain, so they never could take root—though they sprang up quickly enough in the shallow soil. Another handful of seeds hit a patch of thorns that choked the plants as they tried to grow up. Ultimately, however, some seeds took root in good soil and produced a crop.

The Holy Spirit knows that divine appointments take place on all kinds of turf. You don't. So liberally sow and let the crop come up where it may. Be available to the extent that you can be available, as the farmer scattering seeds near and far. Perhaps the deeply ingrained Protestant work ethic makes this laissez-faire approach seem too good to be true. But this is one area in life where sweat equity won't buy you much more than tired muscles.

I needed to remember this last summer as Betty and I vacationed on the jagged Maine coast. Driving home on the Owls Head peninsula, I noticed the low-fuel light blink on. I normally stop at self-serve stations, because my son and son-in-law both own such businesses in Connecticut. But Betty asked me to try a full-serve station nearby where, she claimed, they pumped the gas for the same price.

As I pulled under the station's awning, a man in his late teens hopped out of the building and lifted the pump nozzle almost before I had turned off the car. While the tank filled, he squeegeed the windshield and rubbed off the streaks. I noticed as he leaned over the hood that his name tag read "Angel."

"Is your real name Angel?" I asked through my open window. With a huge smile he nodded. I proceeded to tell him about a television show called *Touched by an Angel* that airs on Sunday nights. I explained that it's about how God helps people handle everyday challenges.

"You should watch it," I added. He asked about the time, and then—almost under his breath—admitted that he could use the help of angels. Due to various brushes with the law, he had lost his driver's license. Without wheels and without much else, the concept of angels hovering brought a measure of comfort and, perhaps, a hint of how God is for him in the time of trouble.

A week after that encounter, I drove by that station several times with a partially empty tank of gas hoping to meet Angel again. But he had flown. Only God knows what became of him. So I must be content knowing I did my part. And that's the way it is with all divine appointments.

In Matthew 28:19, Jesus said, "Go and make disciples." That command didn't change history; the early Christians' obedience to the command changed history.

I recall one Sunday morning when my oldest grand-daughter, Anna, just four, phoned to see if I would pick her up for Sunday school. I asked, "When will you be ready?" Her split-second response was, "I am ready already." The question is, Are we ready already to move? Perhaps a bigger question is, Are we willing to leave the comfort of Fellowship City and move into the broken world of Satansville?

# KEEPING
## APPOINTMENTS

1. What did you think about Bob when he skipped serving Communion in favor of attending a football game with his children?

2. What impression might skipping a church service for this reason leave on his children?

3. Do you sometimes judge people by their attendance and participation in church activities?

4. Should you work out your Christianity in church or in the marketplace?

5. How do these two places differ?

6. What legalisms often creep into church and para-church institutions?

7. What does the concept of "Jesus with skin on" really mean?

8. Do you get uptight about witnessing opportunities? Why or why not?

9. How can you overcome your anxiety about keeping a divine appointment?

10. What percentage of those in your Christian fellowship actively witness?

11. How can you encourage greater openness to witnessing in yourself and others?

12. Do you consider yourself a "cookie-cutter" Christian? Why or why not?

# CHAPTER EIGHT

# VEINS OF SPIRITUAL GOLD

### BY BOB JACKS

*Profoundly speaking, we can never work for God. Jesus takes us over for His enterprises, His building schemes entirely, and no soul has any right to claim where he shall be put.*

—OSWALD CHAMBERS, *MY UTMOST FOR HIS HIGHEST*, MAY 7

*And when [Barnabas] found [Saul], he brought him to Antioch. So for a whole year Barnabas and Saul met with the church and taught great numbers of people. The disciples were called Christians first at Antioch.*

—ACTS 11:26

∾    ∾    ∾

UNDER THE BUBBLE DOME, optic yellow balls whizzed back and forth around the indoor racquet club that mid-December morning. The cavernous setting made each hit sound like a smash.

Heidi Mullane and her friend Debbie, undefeated Connecticut champs in the United States Tennis Association's women's doubles competition the previous summer, had just finished matches on adjacent courts and were about to exchange greetings when Debbie whispered, "I'm not feeling well," and collapsed. In seconds, a place once noisy with the sound of sport—shouts, thwaps, sneakers screeching on the Tupperware-like surface—quieted to nothing more than the whirring ventilation fans.

Deafening ambulance sirens soon filled the air. Momentarily, men in navy uniforms sprinted with a stretcher and medical briefcases toward the anxious group of women. Heidi gathered everyone for prayer as her friend was wheeled away. Debbie, a forty-seven-year-old wife and mother of two, was pronounced dead at the hospital a short while later.

Besides playing tennis that Tuesday, the longtime

doubles partners had a date at Betty's annual Christmas brunch the very next day. Heidi had prepared to share her testimony about finding Christ, and she had invited Debbie to join her. Now Heidi second-guessed her ability to keep the speaking engagement. Could she organize her thoughts enough, given her frayed nerves and heavy heart? Would she be able to speak without blowing through five boxes of Kleenex? Would her pain deflate her passion to proclaim Jesus as a kind and loving God? To find out, she reluctantly kept her appointment with Betty later that afternoon.

## URGENT MATTERS

BETTY EXPECTED Heidi's visit because she likes to be a solo "test audience" the day before anyone shares a testimony at her Christmas brunch. It's not that she produces a staged event at these seeker-sensitive gatherings. It's just that by previewing, she can offer tips on how to stay on track to share in the most effective way possible. But when she heard a light rap on our door, it shocked her to find a deathly pale Heidi staring back with wide, bloodshot eyes.

Between sniffles and strained silences, Heidi explained the tennis court tragedy that had taken place just an hour before. Was it appropriate for her to speak the next day during such an emotional meltdown? Ultimately, the two determined that Debbie's death gave a dimension of urgency to Heidi's testimony.

So besides recounting her own conversion experience, which had taken place a few years earlier in that very same living room, Heidi wove Debbie's sudden death into her testimony as a way to emphasize that no one knows his or her hour. For the unbeliever, she hoped to bring a wake-up call. But believers also do well to remember that time is short. Sometimes God won't give you a second chance to keep a divine appointment.

Furthermore, breaking one divine appointment can theoretically mean breaking many others. Why? God has no grandchildren. Mother Teresa of Calcutta simply stated that we come to Jesus one at a time. For this reason, the church always exists twenty years—just one generation—away from extinction. So every divine appointment kept is a potential key to opening whole new frontiers for God.

Consider those who most influenced you to accept Christ and grow in Him. Then reflect on whom you may later have influenced in the same way. Whether you know it or not, nearly every believer stands like an old-fashioned firefighter passing the same bucket of living water down a line. Those to your right and left may be friends, family members, coworkers, neighbors, or strangers. Nevertheless, they have passed along something precious for you to give to someone else.

## AMEN-HOUR FAMILY CONVERSIONS

IF SHE were alive today, my maternal grandmother could trace long veins of spiritual gold that started with her in the relative isolation of her West Virginia "back forty" plot and then—through me—spread to hundreds of others across the United States and Ukraine. The people affected by this network of faith include family members other than my children. And through some amen-hour conversions, I've learned to remain hopeful about extending the vein of spiritual gold through relatives.

Jobe Kuhl smoked three packs of unfiltered Camels a day and returned from World War II with a purple heart for severe wounds suffered in combat during the Allied invasion of Italy. Yet neither his heavy smoking habit nor his march into harm's way overseas caused him to contemplate his mortality in the light of Christ. It confused me. How could he be so remarkably gentle and kind without faith?

His big heart made me consider him more of an uncle than a distant relative, so naturally I hoped for a divine appointment when he fell ill at a ripe age. My two sons, Michael and Matthew, kept asking me how such an unselfish man like Jobe could escape hell if he never prayed to receive Christ. I mulled this over and over as I raked leaves one afternoon and finally found myself standing by the telephone. Every excuse of why I shouldn't ring him at the hospital in West Virginia—an eleven-hour drive from our home—came to mind. How could I talk with him one last time about faith in Christ? There would surely be nurses hovering around his bed or visitors, right? It could be disruptive.

The Holy Spirit urged me to call, so I dialed his room and soon heard his faint voice on the other end of the line. I had written several letters to him on this subject before I picked up the phone that day, but I wanted to be sure that he understood eternal security. So I explained it again. Then I flat-out asked him if he wanted to invite Christ into his life. I held my breath and listened to the raspy breathing in the receiver. Jobe simply said, "Yes." We sang "Swing Low, Sweet Chariot" at his funeral a few weeks later with tears of joy over his saved life.

I have written other family members similar letters and—long after the ink dried—learned of how those words prepared the reader for a divine appointment with someone else. For instance, as my father-in-law Clyde Smith sat reading my most recent letter one afternoon, a local pastor knocked on his door during a neighborhood visitation. Clyde invited him in and asked him to read the letter too. After skimming it, the pastor asked him if he had ever received Christ. Of course, Clyde said no.

"Would you like to?" the pastor immediately asked. Betty now knows that she will see both of her parents in heaven.

## SALVATION EXCEPTIONS

OF COURSE, some accept Christ without face-to-face contact with a believer. After attending one of our early Lighthouse Bible studies, Bunny Workman wrestled with the Holy Spirit. Then, while cleaning her kitchen floor in absolute solitude, she suddenly threw her mop down.

"Okay, Lord!" she cried in exasperation. "I give up!"

The long-haul trucker may pick up a Christian radio station crossing the Mojave Desert. There's no other soul within miles, much less earshot. Yet he may suddenly accept Christ after decades of rejecting Him. Another person may be walking her dog past a stadium equipped with a booming, outdoor public address system. Perhaps a Billy Graham crusade is in progress and the passerby hears a snippet of truth that touches the softest part of her unbelieving heart. So drawn, the stranger may stick around and pray the sinner's prayer outside the stadium walls.

How about the woman who rushes by the same street preacher parked on the busiest corner of a downtown corporate corridor? One day, her ears may open and she may catch something of God's love that sticks—even after she has marched through three crosswalks since she heard it. Hey, God can work through a circus of circumstances! And all of these folks may genuinely accept Christ and then find fellowship in His church. But these testimonies make the exception, not the rule.

Far more frequently, the good news gets passed from

person to person, divine appointment by divine appointment. Eyes meet, hands shake, words are exchanged. An apple pie is baked and delivered or a greeting card arrives at just the right time. It's a personal introduction to the living Lord. However, I am writing this chapter for two reasons: to show the potential ripple effect just one believer can cause and to encourage believers to see over the shoulder of each divine appointment they keep. Why? *Your influence as a believer extends past a single divine appointment.*

"Although evangelism is personal in response, it is not individual in focus," writes Joseph Aldrich in *Gentle Persuasion*. "Every individual must make a personal decision, but no individual should be viewed in isolation. In other words, I don't go out to 'pick off' individuals. I claim entire networks. I visualize the gospel flowing down webs of relationships, reaching individual after individual who know and are somehow related to each other."[1]

## THE OIKOS PERSPECTIVE

ALDRICH SAYS this view requires an *oikos* perspective. *Oikos,* Greek for "household," is how believers in the early church regarded themselves. They felt part of God's household. With that sense of spiritual family, they could go out to their various circles of influence to share the good news. The Bible shows God using just one person to reach entire households, as eventually was the case with Heidi. Consider the following verses:

> [Cornelius] told us how he had seen an angel appear in his house and say, "Send to Joppa for Simon who is called Peter. He will bring you a message through which you and all your household will be saved." (Acts 11:13-14)

When [Lydia] and the members of her household
were baptized, she invited us to her home. "If
you consider me a believer in the Lord," she said,
"come and stay at my house." (Acts 16:15)

Then Paul left the synagogue and went next door
to the house of Titius Justus, a worshiper of God.
Crispus, the synagogue ruler, and his entire
household believed in the Lord; and many of the
Corinthians who heard him believed and were
baptized. (Acts 18:7-8).

This *oikos* perspective fully supports the concept of
divine appointments. We all have different circles of influence, and those circles are not drawn by accident. Even as
a baby Christian without any evangelism training, Heidi
instinctively took her faith to her household, as you will
soon see. Anyone can do the same.

## ONE VEIN'S COURSE

I CONSIDER the spin-off of divine appointments as *veins
of spiritual gold*. Like the precious metal, one vein can run
deeply through the thickest, hardest rock. For instance,
Heidi is one person in a long vein of spiritual gold Betty
has mined over the years through her Bible studies. Here's
how that particular vein extended.

In 1988, Paige Colantonio attended one of Betty's Bible
studies and eventually renewed her once stagnant faith in
Christ there. And she picked up on a new concept—that
belief wasn't just between her and God. So Paige started
keeping divine appointments with the people in her
world—including those women at the health club where
she exercised. That's where she met Heidi.

Heidi accepted Paige's invitation to Betty's Bible study for a number of reasons. A thirtysomething, stay-at-home mom, Heidi had been quietly fighting a vague unhappiness. Nothing stood out as the culprit. Materially speaking, she could not live any better. But this feeling kept creeping into her life, especially when her husband, David, left her alone with their two sons to go to work or to business-related social events.

With this puzzling undercurrent, Heidi soon picked up on Paige's caring, comforting, and loving attitude toward others. She appreciated the down-to-earth ways this woman related to her in the midst of their somewhat hoity-toity, upper-class Connecticut community. Furthermore, when Heidi checked out the Bible study, she found other women with similar qualities. Though Heidi was churched, no one had ever shared the salvation message with her until then.

## More Steps of Faith

PREOCCUPIED AS he was, David noticed a positive change in Heidi immediately after she came to faith. Looking back, she likens finding new life in Christ to putting on fine new clothing after you've dressed in rags so long. People notice! Eventually, David joined her at one of our couples Bible studies and began to think more about the claims of Christ. Then, during a holiday visit, one of his old partying college buddies led David to faith.

The Mullanes' two preadolescent sons soon followed suit. But Heidi's hopes for her father started fading, even after he was diagnosed with cancer in 1996. Once when he came home from the hospital with a feeding tube, he listened to her testimony about Jesus—but only to please her. He knew so much about the Bible from a childhood spent in Sunday school, but he never took a step of faith.

His stubborn resistance forced Heidi to trust the Lord like never before. She knew she needed a divine appointment infused with a miracle—and fast. God answered that prayer. Shortly before her father died, Heidi and David invited him to the rustic New England brookside baptism of their two sons. They pushed his wheelchair to the water's edge so he could see. There he sat, in suspenders, baggy pants, and a white T-shirt with a photograph of him and Heidi silk-screened on the front. As Trevor (then age ten) and Tyler (then six) came up from the waves dripping and gasping, something must have clicked.

"Don't cry. Don't cry, Heidi," he said after announcing his decision to accept Christ next to his soaked grandsons. "This is the start of my new life."

By the time Heidi's father found Christ, the vein of spiritual gold extended from Betty to Paige to Heidi to David to their two sons to him. That's how God's kingdom develops, through one divine appointment after another.

## POSSIBILITY-LADEN PRAYER

IN OUR ministry, Betty and I regularly pray that our faith will be extended in this way. For instance, when she comes home from her women's Bible study at church, she tells me about newcomers to the group. Betty prays for these women by name. Meanwhile, because Betty and I are on the same team, I pray for the husbands—even when I've never met them or their wives. I've mentioned some of those men in the book: David Mullane, Gary Earl, Kevin Searles, Moe Slayton.

Once a person or family comes into our lives, we stick with them much like a good fisherman sticks with a big fish that he has hooked. Betty and I are passionate about the three Ps of ministry:

∼ Prayer
∼ Patience
∼ Persistence

Over the years, we have found the three Ps critical as we have met and discipled many women like Heidi who eventually bring the good news to every member of their family. We've witnessed the spiritual domino effect that can happen in households, clubs, companies, and every other arena of association.

But that domino effect almost always begins with one divine appointment, and divine appointments can't click where there's no contact between believers and unbelievers. Before you can follow a vein of spiritual gold, you must first find the tip of it by getting into the mine. You have to be willing to go to spiritually dark places where you'll get dirt under your fingernails, dust in your hair, and soot on your clothes.

These places bring Psalm 119:105 to mind: "Your word is a lamp to my feet and a light for my path." Often, hanging out with lost people is like walking on uneven surfaces with only a headlamp to light the path, footstep by footstep.

## No Walls

TO STICK with this rough, off-road course requires getting out of any little box into which you've put yourself. The box around you may be a movement, a religious construct, a legalistic sense of duty, or run-of-the-mill complacency—anything that keeps you from reaching out to share the love of Christ in word and deed.

Penned in, you may lack the availability the Holy Spirit needs to arrange opportunity-laden intersections between you and unbelievers. I met one such believer, a woman named Andi, at a seminar. Her box squished her to the point of depression before she busted the walls. She later sent this letter explaining what it felt like to get out of the box and reach out with an enlarged vision:

I was born into a minister's home and was an only child. I was raised in a very small box, but a box full of love and happiness and security. I liked the box (characterized by a separation or isolation attitude toward "the world" and a legalistic bent of man-made rules for behavior) and would have liked to live and die in the box. The box was comfortable. I could find great meaning in it, and I didn't have the least desire to rebel my way out of it. At 18 years of age, I went to a Christian liberal arts college where I found many wonderful peers who shared my box to one degree or another. I also came into contact with a campus ministry.

After serving full time with the ministry as a single girl for five years, I met Scott—a young but zealous Christian who had never been raised in the box, but who had conformed to the box. Why? He says because "I'd wasted 21 years of my life, I wanted to get serious as a Christian and this was the model I saw." When we married, Scott was a better legalist than I was. I was very happy to share my box with him.

However, as times began to change and as more students were coming to the university with very little religious upbringing and a secular, humanistic perspective, our ministry group began to realize that if we did not change some of our forms (again, man-made) and methods, our objective of making laborers for Christ would, in time, come to a screeching halt.

How could we reach this increasingly lost generation of Baby Boomers and now Baby Busters who generally have no interest in spiritual things—yet who in many cases, are desperately looking for meaning in life and for sincerity, integrity and vulnerability in those who name the name of Christ? There was definitely a need to impact this desperate generation. But as Joseph Aldrich puts it: "There's no impact without contact." And contact demands getting involved in the messiness of others' lives with an attitude of grace, thus moving from *our* comfort zone to *theirs.*

## THE BOLDNESS FACTOR

GETTING OUT of your box to unearth nuggets and even long veins of spiritual gold requires boldness. And boldness, contrary to images of, say, a pushy used-car salesperson, carries a very positive connotation for Christians bringing the message of salvation to those who've never heard. When the early Christians suffered persecution, they prayed for boldness before they prayed for protection: "Now, Lord, consider their threats and enable your servants to speak your word with great boldness" (Acts 4:29).

"Christian boldness is an awesome thing to watch," writes Stephen Brown in *No More Mr. Nice Guy!*

I have seen drug addicts turn from their drugs and alcoholics turn from their bottles because of it. I have seen soldiers cringe in its light. I have seen angry, hostile, abrasive people back away from their plans in the face of it. I have seen sinners repent and saints grow as they are prodded by it. There is something supernaturally powerful about Christian boldness. The problem is that few people have seen that power because not many Christians are willing to exercise it.[2]

One rainy evening when I was feeling a little blue and not so very bold, I sat down to read Brown's book at our kitchen table. Though Betty was working upstairs, she heard me laugh at a story he wrote about a college football team. The score revealed one team as the clear underdog. Yet the losing coach pressed on with his strategies. At one point, he hollered, "Give the ball to Jack! Give the ball to Jack!" However, Jack never got the ball, and the team continued its downward death spiral.

A few minutes later, the coach cupped his hands around his mouth and shouted the same directive: "Give the ball to Jack!" The team had heard his orders the first time. And they may have even felt confident that the play would work. The problem was Jack.

"Jack says he doesn't want the ball!" one player finally yelled back to the coach in exasperation.[3]

I chuckled because that sentiment holds true in keeping divine appointments. Many believers watch the action from the sidelines. Or they stay in the holy huddle always strategizing but never stepping out on the field and getting into the game. Others run around, but they're not really interested in carrying the ball—so they drop it.

That's okay. God loves you even if you don't lift a finger to show and tell His love to unbelievers. However, remember that God never wastes time. He doesn't waste His time, and He won't waste your time by giving you mistaken divine appointments. If you sense an opportunity to share, be bold enough to trust that it's orchestrated by the Holy Spirit and that you can act on that prompting—regardless of what results.

A few years ago, a white Honda pulled up beside my car. I looked over my shoulder and recognized Arlene Brazinski—one of the hairdressers Betty has led to Christ. She poked her head out and invited me to join her and her friend Barb Wesley for a cup of coffee. I soon learned that Barb was married to Glen Wesley, a member of the then-Hartford Whalers National Hockey League team. Several of his teammates already attended our church, and the congregation took great care in giving them space and privacy. But Barb asked me to draw closer to her and her husband through prayer. She had already accepted Christ. He had not.

Boldness means daring to pray for high-flyers like Glen. So I penciled his name on the credit-card-sized list I keep in my wallet, and in this way I remembered to pray for him often. Glen later accepted Christ at our church, and I count that a special blessing because he then began sharing his testimony with boldness even though public speaking unnerved him at the time. And he continues to boldly share his faith with his teammates—now the Carolina Hurricanes, since the Whalers relocated. The Wesleys also host a Lighthouse Bible study at their home in North Carolina.

As you become more aware of divine appointments and ask God for a higher level of blessing and influence among the lost, remember Jabez's prayer (see 1 Chronicles 4:9-10). That prayer reflects a man humbled by his own limited abilities, but hoping in God's infinite resources.

## OPPORTUNITIES ON THE BUS

LIMITED. THAT was exactly how I felt when my plane touched down in Denver a couple of years ago. For starters, the flight from Connecticut to Colorado takes a chunk of time, given the transfers. Furthermore, after I had spent what seemed to be light-years waiting at the baggage carousel, I figured my suitcases had taken a trip of their own—perhaps to Brazil. I shuddered at the thought of a last-minute shopping spree for everything from toothpaste to ties.

To compound the problem, I was frustrated with myself for flying to Denver in the first place instead of flying directly to Colorado Springs where my meetings would be held. So in a grumpy, defeated mood, I trudged to the counter to file my luggage claim. Then, miraculously, my bags surfaced in a back room. I sprinted to catch the bus to my rental car. Glancing at my watch, I couldn't help but mutter that I could have been in Colorado Springs by now.

But God knew why I made that decision, and the Holy Spirit had already lined up a divine appointment for me aboard that bus. As I clung to an overhead bar in the crowded vehicle, I noticed a young couple sitting on the back seat watching their preschool-age daughter restlessly rocking back and forth between them. I struck up a conversation by asking about their destination, which turned out to be Aspen. Yet, despite the luxury accommodations and world-class skiing that awaited these Floridians, they seemed distracted and glum.

As their daughter continued looking like she was missing her favorite doll, I thought of my own granddaughters because they were about the same age. Then, for some reason, I asked the couple if they had any other children. That's when their eyes filled with tears and the story spilled out during the short trip from the terminal to the parking lot. Their youngest daughter, two-year-old Courtney, had drowned in their swimming pool just two weeks prior, and nothing seemed to help them shake the sorrow that had enveloped them since her death.

Whoa! In the midst of my rotten day choked with roadblocks, the Holy Spirit graciously opened a door. All I could think to say was, "Do you mind if I pray for you?" That's the only response that seemed appropriate as I looked at the brokenhearted couple. Soon we were forced to part ways, but I boldly asked for their address and kept in touch to encourage them and pray for them.

As I pulled the seat belt across my chest in the rental car, I began to weep. What if that tragedy had struck my four-year-old granddaughter, Anna? It could have been her clinging to her parents' knees and shifting to and fro in vague confusion had she lost her younger sister Grace. For those few minutes, the Lord put me in that family's shoes. He prompted me to pray for them. Still, I wondered if I could have done or said more.

I'm not sure how God can use this divine appointment as an entrée to a whole other network of people. But when they responded to my correspondence, I felt affirmed for being bold about Christ.

## THE LETTER

DEAR BOB, thank you so very much for your lovely letter. You truly are a poet and we absorbed all of your heartfelt words and prayers. When my husband [John] and I read your letter, we both were so touched that we cried and couldn't believe that a total stranger was so kind and had gone to such great lengths to try and reach us to express your concern and prayers.

I will be honest in saying that our lives are truly taken moment-by-moment and day-by-day. We have good days and quite a few bad days. We're just hoping that time will be a bit kinder and gentler to us and hopefully [will] have better things in store for us in the future. There isn't a day that goes by and we don't think of her. Of course, I always wonder how she would be right now. How big, how much talking or just working [with] Mommy in her [own] way. She was always a little handful. Alexandra misses her terribly. They both shared a bedroom together. Courtney, our youngest that drowned, was always the more outgoing, initiator, and more precocious. Alexandra is now three-and-a-half [and] is more shy and introverted, especially now.

John and I normally don't tell strangers our grief. But when we met you on the bus, your most common question of asking us if we had other children had taken us by surprise, and that is why we reacted as such. And, thankfully for us, we met a wonderful, kind man. So something good came from this. . . . We hope you and your whole family are well and will have a great Easter.

Because I am not a poetic writer, I believe the same Holy Spirit who penned the Bible through ordinary people penned the letter to this couple. Paul's letters changed history. A letter you write could be used to change the destiny of a person.

I'm not sure where this family is in relationship to Christ. They reacted positively to the way I reached out to them. However, chances are that I will lose contact and never know the work God could do in them and through them to reach others. Part of being bold means putting the outcomes in His hands.

Before you get into your own unique divine appointments, you've got to get out of the box enough to do God's math. God's math? Consider this. A boxed-in, cookie-cutter Christian may envision a boxed-in, cookie-cutter God—a

God with prescribed dimensions who stamps out predictable results based on those dimensions.

The psalmist wrote, "Blessed are those whose strength is in you [God], who have set their hearts on pilgrimage" (Psalm 84:5). By definition, pilgrimages mean striking out past familiar borders and remaining flexible in the face of unknowns. If you seek and keep only those divine appointments that add up to what you perceive as realistic—that align with your sense of possibility and ambition—you'll shortchange yourself and who knows how many others in another person's world. (And don't forget the concept of relaxed anticipation from chapter 7.)

God told an incredulous Abraham, "I will surely bless you and make your descendants as numerous as the stars in the sky and as the sand on the seashore. Your descendants will take possession of the cities of their enemies, and through your offspring all nations on earth will be blessed, because you have obeyed me" (Genesis 22:17-18) In a sense, this promise of physical progeny applies to spiritual progeny. Through it, can you catch a glimpse of God's crazy math—His uncanny way of multiplying blessings for the bold and the faithful?

# KEEPING
## APPOINTMENTS

1. How would you describe a "vein of spiritual gold"?

2. How do you get out of the box to start this type of vein?

3. Would you feel comfortable praying Jabez's prayer for enlarged territory (1 Chronicles 4:9-10)?

4. Do you have family members who have not

accepted Christ? How could you begin to reach out to them?

5. How would you have interacted with the grieving couple riding the rental car bus?

6. Do you know many people who, like Jack, shirk catching the ball and running with it?

7. How can you get to a place where you want to catch the ball and run with it? How can you encourage others to do likewise?

# CHAPTER NINE

# SIDE BY SIDE

## BY BOB JACKS

*Our work as His disciples is to disciple lives until they are wholly yielded to God. One life wholly devoted to God is of more value to God than one hundred lives simply awakened by His Spirit.*

—OSWALD CHAMBERS, *MY UTMOST FOR HIS HIGHEST*, APRIL 24

*Flee the evil desires of youth, and pursue right-eousness, faith, love and peace, along with those who call on the Lord out of a pure heart.*

—2 Timothy 2:22

∽  ∽  ∽

A S GALES OF BLOWING snow drifted over the lonely stretch of Maine highway near our favorite vacation spot, I hunkered over the steering wheel and fretted. Despite all the careful prearrangements and my penchant for punctuality, I figured I'd miss meeting Kirk at the New Hampshire coffee shop by a lousy thirty minutes. What a shame.

According to my daughter's friend and former brides-maid, Brady—the person who suggested we meet—Kirk had been searching, but needed more guidance to find Christ. A forty-one-year-old trust-funder, he had chucked work indefinitely to build a three-thousand-square-foot log cabin amid New Hampshire's pines. Would I meet him en route to Connecticut?

By another generous act of God, I pulled into the small parking lot only five minutes off my ETA. The problem then turned inside out. Would Kirk be on time, given the blizzardlike conditions?

The wafting aroma of fresh-brewed coffee and just-out-of-the-oven cinnamon rolls met me at the door. I scanned the quaint bakery/gift shop for a man wearing a tan Carhartt jacket and spotted him in a snap that day, November 20, 2000. After all, young women sipping lattes dominated the clientele.

I learned that despite all my fretting, I had nothing to worry about. He had taken a seat early and never questioned that I'd show up, even during Mother Nature's chilly temper tantrum. He planned to camp out there with a bottomless coffee carafe until I stumbled in from the cold.

Because we glossed over small talk about the storm almost as soon as I slid in across from him, I asked one of my favorite entry-point questions: "Where are you on your journey through life?" Right off the bat, Kirk confessed that he needed guidance—especially in the area of guilt. His good fortune in business only compounded those feelings of unworthiness.

As I probed for more details, he explained that even without a boss riding him or the pressure of earning a paycheck, he obsessed about productivity. He worried about wasting time and energy. What's more, he felt deeply conflicted and guilty over his relationship to his father. The man abused alcohol and Kirk. Kirk couldn't forgive. But he also couldn't forget, and it felt like a Chinese water droplet torture on his soul.

## A CLOSER LOOK

AS I peeled back other layers of the onion, I learned that Kirk first heard the gospel at age four. He also told me that his mother read the Bible to him and his four brothers and sisters before the family went to Sunday school. They even prayed together up until about his tenth birthday. Then, for unclear reasons, they stopped. His church attendance also nose-dived two years later when he enrolled at a distant boarding school.

This is a familiar story for so many. They have enough spiritual background to make them hungry for God, but not enough support to meet that need with Christ. In this regard, Kirk was a textbook case. He rebelled. He feigned a hip disaffection. He lived the high life. But his thoughts circled around the gospel more often than he let on. He had retained the spiritual curiosity he felt as a youngster.

So he restlessly continued seeking—more or less—through it all. He periodically pondered questions like, If there is a God, and if Jesus Christ really did come back to life, how could He have lived here and still been so pure and righteous?

Furthermore, Kirk assumed that part of being a good person meant modeling some Christian tenets. So he tried to be helpful, truthful, and unselfish. But without the real thing, without Christ and a Christian mentor, he feared he'd be in bondage to the same struggles and confusion, decade after decade.

After about three coffee refills, when he had detailed the ups and downs of his searching, I shared my fifteen-minute testimony and highlighted several of my most defining moments as a Christian. He listened intently. Looking back, he began realizing how he had tried to fill the God-shaped part of his heart with all sorts of pricey toys and activities.

"Sounds like you're missing just one thing, Kirk," I eventually said, sitting back in my chair and folding my arms.

"What's that?" he replied. Then the lights came on in his eyes, and he confessed that it was God. It took more frank conversation to convince him that he was worthy of God's grace and forgiveness, because he felt terribly selfish. Yet Kirk prayed to accept Christ as the snow swirled outside.

## LONG-DISTANCE DISCIPLESHIP

THOUGH HE lives five hours from my home, I now disciple Kirk. Why would I pour that kind of effort into someone so far from my zip code? Without discipleship, side-by-side accountability, and encouragement, Kirk could stray from his newfound convictions—"wander from the ranch," as we often say.

So before parting ways on that blustery November day, Kirk and I agreed to talk once a week. During our meetings, we have completed Bill Bright's workbook, *The Christian Adventure.* (I recommended the book because it covers the basics of the Christian life including prayer, Bible study, fellowship, worship, and evangelism.) We are now halfway through the workbook *The Christian and the Holy Spirit.*

Kirk continued worrying about the skeletons in his closet, so I suggested that he write down his sins, pray for forgiveness, and then burn the paper. I also encouraged him to call on Jesus to answer the door to his heart when the Devil knocks. We found a great local church for him to attend, because Bible studies and discipleship partnerships make a supplement, not a substitute.

Consequently, Kirk often shares his insights on the previous Sunday's sermon. I regularly ask him for application examples. For instance, one Sunday-morning message dealt with acceptance and forgiveness—two themes that strike heavy chords in his troubled relationship with his father. Kirk told me his pastor highlighted Romans 12:17-21, 15:1-7, and Ephesians 4:32 to illustrate how forgiving others and striving to build up one another in Christ glorifies God. This made for rich conversation and initiated a new growth process for him to churn through.

"My siblings have wondered why I have been moved to help my father, in spite of his hurting me, as he has hurt us all over the years," he wrote in a recent e-mail.

I now understand my heart has been and is being moved by the Lord. . . . Having accepted

Him into my life, I feel I can better reach out to my father. I pray that my relationship with Dad will grow and that my siblings, despite their own feelings toward him, will understand this is what I must do. . . . I pray that my siblings, too, will come to see that forgiveness and acceptance is right for my father, as it is for us all.

## FROM SCRATCH

MATTHEW 28:19-20 states, "Go and make disciples of all nations, baptizing them in the name of the Father and of the Son and of the Holy Spirit, and teaching them to obey everything I have commanded you. And surely I am with you always, to the very end of the age." To me, the operative word in this verse is not "go." If you've gotten this far in the book, you're probably ready, willing, and more able to go than what is even necessary. So the operative word in my mind is "make." If step one means going, step two means rolling up your sleeves and making—discipling—another believer who can in turn disciple someone else to disciple someone else.

Many believers envision these relationships unfolding in a church setting where they meet a wanderer who needs more support in grasping solid biblical theology or practicing the Christian lifestyle. That's good. Yet, to me, making a disciple means starting from the ground up with an unbeliever. Kirk fits into this category of discipleship.

It's a time-consuming process that reminds me of making bread from scratch. My daughter, Beth, serves mostly homemade food. Years before the nifty bread makers hit store shelves, she took time to mix the dough, knead it, let it rise, pop it in the oven, and finally slice it for the table. When Betty and I join her family for dinner, I remind my son-in-law that he really has it good. What other man in Simsbury, Connecticut—at least in the pre-bread-maker era—could watch butter melt on homemade, fresh-baked bread?

When Beth pulls the red-and-white gingham cloth from the loaf nestled in its basket, it looks picture-perfect—a cover shot for *Better Homes and Gardens*. But if you peeked around the corner at the kitchen, you could see the trappings of what it took to produce it. The mess includes a huge mixing bowl with leftover glue-like dough stuck inside, flour dusted on the rolling board and some sprinkled on the floor, pans greased with Crisco, and a hot oven. A fully baked loaf of bread takes no small amount of time and energy.

## HUNGER PAINS

CALLING KIRK week after week, praying for him, and teaching him how to pray—in short, caring for him—requires time and energy. Still, I consider it an investment, not a sacrifice, because divine appointments without discipleship miss what Jesus modeled before His first followers. He listened. He taught and encouraged. He walked the talk, day after day. He changed the world by feeding those men the ways and means to truth. Then He commanded them to go and do likewise.

In John 21, the resurrected Jesus emphasized this when He finished eating breakfast with His disciples. Three times He made a simple "if-then" statement—if you love Me, then feed My sheep—in a repetitive teaching style common in elementary school.

When my cousin Ted Crew and I opened our truck stop east of Hartford on I-84, we dug around in shoeboxes and trunks for old family photographs. We then enlarged and framed them to display on the walls of our new business. I kept one of those photos in my home office after we sold out, because it reminded me of discipleship.

Framed in bright red, this black-and-white shot shows my Grandmother Crew in her aproned work dress and me standing bare-chested before the dilapidated house she called home. Hers was a scratch farm to be sure. So good thing she lived in West Virginia, where almost everyone's related to everyone else, however distantly. For this reason, the community looked out for her as best they could during those tough Depression and war years.

For instance, they always gave her their sick or weak lambs. If she could nurse them to health and maturity, she could sell their wool. In the photo, we must have been busy doing just that kind of nurturing. I hold a tin can with the grain feed in it. But she, so characteristically, feeds a little lamb with a jumbo milk bottle.

## UNTAPPED POWER?

MY PHILOSOPHY on discipleship is stark. If you don't keep divine appointments and make disciples, you will fall heartbreakingly short of your spiritual growth and ministry potential.

In *Holy Sweat,* Tim Hansel recalls an episode of the *Merv Griffin Show* that illustrates the folly of power without usage. The guests that night included a group of bodybuilders who looked like they could rip down the Empire State Building with their bare hands. They were modern Samsons.

When Merv recovered from his unblinking assessment of their impeccable physiques, he shuffled his papers and inquired about the functionality of their brawn. One of the men silently responded by striking a pose, his taunt muscles visibly feathering underneath the fat-free covering of skin.

"'No, you don't understand me,' Merv said. 'What do you *use* all those muscles for?'

"The guy said, 'I'll show you.' And he flexed again, posing in another way.

"'No. No. You still don't understand my question. Read my lips. What do you *use* them for?' And the guy posed again."[1]

## Hard Truths

PEOPLE LIKE Barb don't benefit from contact with Christian posers. They need contact with authentic disciples who will meet them with the love of Christ. This can be a taller order than it seems.

When Russ Maida met Barb at the insurance company where they both worked, he had no idea that she struggled with depression serious enough to ultimately require an extended medical leave. He never suspected the turmoil roiling just beneath her carefully applied makeup, spotless glasses, well-brushed long hair, and fitted suit. After all, Barb acted like the savvy corporate training developer she was—confident, funny, smart, and innovative.

Privately, however, she considered her life an exercise in futility, an endless game of recklessly driving down one dead-end road after another looking for love. Along the way, she found plenty of facsimiles—in romantic relationships, drugs, her career. But the pit of lovelessness in her stomach remained.

Looking back, she thinks this ache started during her early childhood when she internalized the hard news— that she was no one's only one. With eight other children in the family, she constantly scrapped for attention and always failed to get enough of it. Then she married and expected more love—not less. But after fifteen years of emotional abuse, she divorced due to the yawning greatness of the deficit. That's when tremendous waves of disillusionment washed over her and suicide seemed as close as the medicine chest.

When Russ spotted his coworker on the soccer field where both of their kids played one Saturday morning, he struck up a conversation. Though Russ was oblivious of her dire circumstances, God led him to invite her to a Lighthouse Bible study. Barb accepted, thinking she had nothing to lose. There, she learned more about the love, forgiveness, and hope she needed in her life. After accepting Christ through the Bible study, she needed to be discipled.

## THROUGH THICK AND THIN

MOTHER TERESA once said, "Everything is God's to give and to take away, so share what you've been given, and that includes yourself."[2] When Diane, Russ's wife, discovered Barb's troubles, she could have opted out. Instead she drew near like my grandmother did with the struggling little lambs. Through this discipleship relationship, Diane helped Barb plug into Betty's weekly women's Bible study. Those women eventually watched Barb take the giant step back to work and a fully functioning lifestyle.

Barb had lost her faith in her twenties before she ever fully claimed it. Her spiritual shrinkage started when a skeptic in her world scoffed at the way she was warming to the notion of a powerful God.

"What makes you think that there's a God?" she remembers him taunting. With no ready answers and no Christian community to catch her as she lost her balance, Barb started a freefall. Her misgivings about life crested around the time she met Diane. Barb had just turned forty and scheduled a routine baseline physical. Oddly, she never expected her doctor to tell her she was "flirting with danger." Until then, her blues seemed typical. But he confirmed the clinical nature of her depression and warned her to get help immediately.

Soon, dressed in a hospital gown and slippers, she sat for ten days on the suicide-watch floor and considered him prophetic. For the next three months, Barb took a leave of absence from work and experimented with various antidepressants and support-group therapy as an outpatient. During this tough time, she bitterly noted that not one of her colleagues sent a card, called, or wired flowers.

When the clinic released Barb, Diane showed up with an Italian dinner—lasagna, salad, croutons, the works—for Barb and her children to enjoy. She also called for progress checks. Later she invited Barb to our church's annual Christmas brunch. That year, six hundred women turned out to hear one of our ministry teammates, Jessica Stewart, speak. Her message revolved around the concept of God giving us a wrapped gift, and that you've not really received it until you open it. This helped Barb understand that what she had done when she accepted Christ at the Bible study was only the beginning of the journey.

So for four solid weeks, Diane spent her lunch hour discipling a severely depressed, out-of-work single mom who figured she could as much afford to hope in opening that gift as she could afford to turn the key of a Mercedes Benz. Yet reading John 1–6 with Diane over soup and sandwiches awakened Barb's spiritual appetite. She soon devoured the rest of the New Testament and started praying to open the gift of faith to see how it would work in her crazy life.

Barb's counselor had encouraged everyone in the support group to do one tiny task outside of the comfort zone, probably something they enjoyed doing before they sank into their depression. Some of the women visited their manicurists. Others went shopping. Surprisingly, Barb just wanted to go to church. As she seat-belted her kids into the car on Sunday morning, she anticipated a hailstorm of sharp judgment the second she darkened the door, because she still lived recklessly. Nevertheless, Barb pulled into a church parking lot. Then, in a cold sweat, she peeled out just as quickly.

Most churchgoing believers cannot relate to the anxiety that surrounds questions like, Will someone greet me? How long does the service last? Will my kids fidget too much in the pew? Will I know when to sit and stand? Will I have to identify myself as a visitor? Given those unknowns, I can understand why seekers often dread attending church. That underscores the power of more informal contacts and "off campus" discipleship.

When Barb reported her weekend activity to the support group, they were in the know. They never asked, "What's up with that? You didn't go into the service? Why not?" Nope. Instead they were mellow. All they said of her swing through was, "Great, great." And guess what? Diane projected the same attitude—even as she discipled Barb with New Testament teaching. With this kind of gentle, persistent love, Diane at last witnessed Barb walking through the church doors, both literally and figuratively.

## PROGRESS PURSUITS

DR. MARTIN Luther King Jr. once admitted, "I may not be the man I want to be; I may not be the man I ought to be; I may not be the man I could be; I may not be the man I can be; but praise God, I'm not the man I once was."[3] Discipleship relationships provide a backdrop upon which to note this kind of evolution and outlook.

The discipleship Christ modeled works in business too.

My mailbox gets stuffed with magazines and newsletters aimed at efficiency, productivity, and quality. On those pages I read that while mentoring takes a significant time investment, companies with mentoring programs target quality control at its most fundamental level—the human resource level. Of course, the trades have always featured apprenticeship. And athletic teams rarely gel well without a coach. Now corporate America's on the bandwagon, and the following tips from that sector help me go about my business better for God as well. Using these same guidelines will help others become disciples. [4]

~ *Practice good listening skills.* Try to listen more than you talk.

~ *Ask questions.* An important part of good listening involves asking Socratic-type questions that will help someone really think through the situation and also the possible consequences of his or her actions. You should also ask questions based in simple curiosity, questions that get behind the issues. . . . Avoid asking "why" questions. They can sound judgmental and may provoke a defensive response.

~ *Be willing to give up control.* Acting as a mentor isn't a matter of telling the other person what to do, but of providing guidance and counsel and then letting that person make his or her own decisions.

~ *Give the relationship time.* Prepare for a commitment of at least two years. Much of the first year will be devoted to climbing a steep learning curve as the two of you learn what to expect of the relationship and of each other.

~ *Don't pretend you're perfect.* Be ready to openly discuss the problems and frustrations you've faced. . . . This will help build trust and rapport between the two of you.

~ *Be prepared to be blunt.* While an individual may expect moral support in anything he or she chooses to do, you're not living up to your responsibility as a mentor by simply telling that person whatever he or she wants to hear.

～ *Remember that actions speak louder than words.* If you counsel on doing the right thing instead of the convenient thing, be sure you practice the same behavior.

## WALK THE TALK

THIS LAST point reminds me of when my partner Ted Crew and I ran the truck stop. Part of the corporate structure included an award program that identified excellence in five areas of truck-stop management on an annual basis. When we first earned the award, it set a standard for the managers and staff to uphold. But I quickly realized that talking about the standard would never be inspiring enough. Rather, I needed to model my high expectations by doing the dirtiest low-down job at the place.

Swishing the toilets? No. Scrubbing the grills? No. Washing the windows? No. My personal pet peeve and all-time grunt job on the premises was picking up cigarette butts. Yet every time I spotted one on our sidewalks or in the halls, I kneeled down and gingerly removed it. Why? If I do it, our managers will do it. If they do it, the staff will do it. People imitate their leaders. That is why Jesus Christ and the first-century church leaders concentrated so much of their time and energy on winning people for the Lord and making disciples.

To interest an ordinary believer in taking the next step and becoming a disciple, I lead by

～ maintaining a solid total commitment to Jesus Christ,

～ bringing a servant attitude to the relationship,

～ praying regularly for those I disciple,

～ maintaining a sense of humor, smiling, and keeping it fun,

- understanding that doubt, frustration, and failures are part of the process,
- encouraging progress and gradually raising the bar,
- presenting a clear picture of our goals,
- teaching that person how to share his or her personal testimony in five, fifteen, and thirty minutes,
- showing that person how to lead someone to Christ,
- determining that person's spiritual gifts and giving opportunities to use those gifts,
- explaining how he or she can disciple someone, and
- being accessible to those I disciple. They can call me at home or work, anytime.

## SIMPLE AVAILABILITY

THAT WRITTEN, remember you do not need a paint-by-number approach to discipleship or a portfolio of church/parachurch involvement to be effective. I meet many men and women who worry about dotting the i's and crossing the t's in their lay ministries. But that's not critical. Availability is. With Christ's love in your life and some or all of the above leadership qualities, you're ready to reach out—to say "yes" to the divine appointments and discipleship opportunities God brings your way.

In chapter 5, I introduced you to Michelle, the young woman who works at my son-in-law's gas station and recently accepted Christ. With less than a year's worth of faith, this quiet woman reached out to Ellen. Ellen had just moved to Simsbury to resettle after her fourteen-year marriage dissolved.

"A year and a half earlier, I was just this nice little person with a gourmet group and a kids play group," Ellen shares. "The only trauma I had to deal with was what wallpaper I needed to pick for the bathroom."

But in the wake of a thorny divorce, Ellen often showed up at the gas station for coffee and biscotti, a grown woman who felt she had no place else to go, no one with whom to say "Hello" and "How are you?" At that point of her greatest social disconnect, the interpreter for the deaf and special education teacher knew she needed to regularly wake up from her grief-stricken stupor.

She joined a divorce support group at church, but the gas station turned out to be her little haven, the mecca to meet other people working through their problems with God's help. Michelle, for one, sympathized with Ellen and kept encouraging her as she brewed coffee for the ten air pots she stocks. For instance, when Ellen missed a Bible study, Michelle would say she missed Ellen there. Most importantly, Michelle simply offered a listening ear and friendly acceptance when Ellen showed up to get away from life's woes for a moment.

With pastors so overworked, overwhelmed, and understaffed, the church needs laity like Michelle to step in to minister in practical ways throughout the week. Discipleship may be highly structured, as was the case when Diane met with Barb over lunch every day for a month. Or it may be casual, as is the support Michelle extends to Ellen when she drops by for coffee. Regardless, in both situations, there's mutually beneficial progress in strengthening the kingdom of God—one person at a time.

# KEEPING
## APPOINTMENTS

1. Have you ever experienced a one-on-one discipleship relationship? How did you benefit from that relationship?

2. Does your church have a healthy discipleship ministry?

3. What do you think of the "starting from scratch" approach to making disciples?

4. What are the advantages of discipling a seeker or new believer versus a longtime Christian?

5. Where were all the Christians during Barb's struggles?

6. How can you reach out to those facing difficult circumstances?

7. Would you feel comfortable discipling others through Bob's approach?

# CHAPTER TEN

# STUMBLING BLOCKS AND STEPPING-STONES

### BY BOB JACKS

*When the Spirit of God has shed abroad the love of God in our hearts, we begin deliberately to identify ourselves with Jesus Christ's interests in other people, and Jesus Christ is interested in every kind of man there is.*

—OSWALD CHAMBERS, *MY UTMOST FOR HIS HIGHEST,* FEBRUARY 24

*Though I am free and belong to no man, I make myself a slave to everyone, to win as many as possible.*

—1 Corinthians 9:19

❧   ❧   ❧

ONE BUILDING, LIKE ONE life, can look relatively unchanged on the outside even after a gutting takes place on the inside. Such is the case with our men's 6 A.M. Bible study venue. Every Friday, fifteen to twenty of us gather in a weather-beaten gray barn planted in the rolling countryside that surrounds Simsbury. But it's not really a barn. In the middle of the twentieth century, the Presbyterians rehabbed it into a church.

Inside, knotty pine pews now butt up against walls once lined with New England dairy cow stanchions. A geometric mosaic of stained glass covers the loft window to the rear through which a farmer once hauled countless sweet-smelling hay bales. And thick, broad rafters crisscross high above to support the traditional barn roof pitches. But as far as I can tell, the swallows and the mice left with the grain, and the renovation neutralized any lingering barn odors.

Now, in the dead of winter—decades after that summer when men in bib overalls drove the timber pillars, nailed the planks, and slapped the first roof on the barn—I enter the church in casual dress. It's 5:45 A.M., milking time in yesteryear. Today, though, the only things we'll be milking are two pots of gourmet coffee. By 6:05, most of the men lean back in their folding chairs, rubbing the cobwebs from their eyes and sipping themselves into greater wakefulness.

Contrary to these opening phases of our gathering, we're not a reserved bunch. These walls hadn't heard anything—from the moos to the hymns—until we started meeting here in 1999. (This was our back porch Bible study, but due to its steady growth we had to move it to a larger facility.) I half joke with my wife that our Friday morning men's klatch is the holy of holies, that we silently file into the room like monks cupping candles through the predawn darkness for confession and prayer. She knows that we in fact come from different denominations and socioeconomic levels. Yet, even without the uniformity of hooded brown robes, hemp belts, and shaven heads, we share the same passion—getting more serious about seeking God and reaching out to the lost.

## AN INSIDE JOB

ONE MEMBER explains that the group gives him the courage to look in the mirror. Then, instead of polishing the outside, he feels challenged to bulldoze the junk inside and ask Jesus the carpenter to reconstruct the site. Without long-term analysis, his external appearance might change imperceptibly. He may cinch the same ties around his neck every morning, eat eggs over-easy as before, hug the same family, and jog the same loop around his neighborhood.

Yet, like the barn, the purpose of his existence has changed profoundly. Instead of common aspirations and energies, a measure of sacredness now fills the space of who he is. To be in God's service, he doesn't need to go— as in pack, pick up, and move—anywhere. If he unlocks the security gates around his life and keeps his lamp of faith trimmed and burning for Christ, the Holy Spirit will send the mission field to him, usually one person at a time.

In New England, where reportedly only 5 to 10 percent of the population know Christ personally, God's got a vast pool from which to pick. So our group decided to operate as missionaries in this place, the place we call home. The great thing is that we can drink the water, speak the language, and don't need to raise financial support. I challenge anyone transformed within by Christ to view his or her surroundings in the same light.

Hurrah! For years I feared that giving God carte blanche availability would shrink my options to precisely two: overseas ministry or seminary. My enthusiasm withered at the thought of those paths of obedience. Now I know better. God needs people, even theologically uneducated people, to respond to the sharing opportunities He presents in every nook and cranny of creation—from a grocery checkout line in Columbus to a hut meeting in the Congo. Humbly handing God a new heart and an open calendar means as much as handing Him a change-of-address card—though He may ask that at some point along your spiritual journey. You let go; He chooses.

## GOD'S PR PERSON

AS THE inkiness outside lightens to a liturgical-looking purple, we settle into our circle with the endgame in mind—encouraging greater accountability, spiritual stability, and, ultimately, availability for divine appointments. It's a tall order, given the many cultural cues to cloak faith. We live in the new "don't ask, don't tell" age, and religion continues to make the "Top Three" list of conversational faux pauxs—it's still right up there with politics and sex. So when I meet divine appointments, I intentionally avoid bringing up "religion" per se in favor of discussing "God things."

Even with the support of a tight-knit accountability group, a bright inside-out faith, and less negatively charged language, many things will tempt you to limit the kind of availability that welcomes divine appointments. So I will use this final chapter to address key stumbling blocks—heartbreakers and failures I've learned in thirty-seven years of field experience—and to point out some solid stepping-stones, which begin with a sense of being blessed to bless and end with simply expecting more mystery and excitement.

## HEARTBREAKERS

MAKE NO mistake. The results of keeping divine appointments and making disciples taste bittersweet. Why? Because sooner or later, letting God use you to plant, nurture, or harvest the seeds of faith will break your heart and could cause you to stumble in your own walk with Christ. After all, if your relationship with Him is personal, rejection will feel that way too—even though, in reality, Jesus Christ always stands as the true fall guy. The scorn is about Him, not you, and that's nothing new.

Even so, many disappointments and even flat-out humiliations visit transparent believers willing to share the gospel in word and deed. After one of our home Bible studies, we held an open house. Guests could wander all over. That night, Betty noticed that a prized ring had vanished from her jewelry box. When I gave paperback New Testaments to a construction crew several summers back, one man turned and urinated on his copy. You put your life into people, and then they stop returning your calls— or worse. These sound mild compared to what Christians and missionaries suffer in other parts of the globe. Even so, these small things sometimes cause discouragement.

World Vision founder Bob Pierce lived by the motto: "May my heart break with the things that break the heart of God."[1] You need not look far and wide or long and hard to find heartbreakers. Note that the rudest responses invariably come from those wounded by the church or rebelling against God. A few such women have barged out of Betty's study and accused her of narrow-mindedness as they grabbed their stuff. Another started balancing a Bible on her head like a bored six-year-old as Betty spoke to her about forgiveness. This woman would then let the Bible slide off and bounce on the table.

But the irreverence of acquaintances only stings when compared with bites from those with whom you're more involved. For instance, when Bryan Marcoux—the former Mafia man—converted to Christianity, he kept his Harley Davidson and returned to his old stomping grounds to share the good news with his former cronies. Through Bryan, we met and ministered to ex-cons and drug addicts who often desperately needed employment and housing in addition to spiritual mentoring.

Two guys stand out: Eric and Billy. In chapter 7, I mentioned Billy's battle to get clean and stay clean—something he finally accomplished at David Wilkerson's rehab center after two yearlong stints. Eric, on the other hand, sat behind bars again on fresh charges just a few months after his release (although he's now out of jail again and making progress).

It broke our hearts. Naturally, we hoped he would lay hold of the gospel and allow Christ to change him from the inside out. Situations like this will sorely tempt you to write off the invested time, money, energy, and prayer as a total loss—a big fat zero contribution in the kingdom of God. We also struggled with the urge to get gun shy and to steer clear of outreach that seemed sketchy from the get-go. Ultimately, we overcame this clunky stumbling block by trusting God to work it out according to His crazy economy and alternative clock.

Like Jesus, believers who go public plow some hard ground, thanks to the hard-hearted human condition. The apostle Paul recognized the difficulty of this ministry in 2 Corinthians 4:8-9: "We are hard pressed on every side, but not crushed; perplexed, but not in despair; persecuted, but not abandoned; struck down, but not destroyed."

Yet these verses hint at a tenacious hope. Good thing, because if you're passionate about anything—even about rooting for a sports team—you will take some hits. And the depth of your heartache directly correlates to the depth of your love for unbelievers, the extent to which you let Christ soften and reshape your heart into a bigger one more like His. By faith allow Christ to love others through you.

Joseph Aldrich writes, "Love them until they ask us why."[2] Indeed, sharing the uncommon love of Christ raises eyebrows, turns heads, and redeems the woefully way-ward. It also hurts at times. However, like it or not, the heartbreakers will help you identify more deeply with the Man of sorrows. Jesus knew plenty of heartache because He gave plenty of love.

In *The Four Loves*, C. S. Lewis warned about the consequences of loving—and not loving:

> To love at all is to be vulnerable. Love anything, and your heart will certainly be wrung and possibly broken. If you want to make sure of keeping it intact, you must give your heart to no one, not even to an animal. Wrap it carefully round with hobbies and little luxuries; avoid all entanglements; lock it up safe in the casket or coffin of your selfishness. But in that casket—safe, dark, motionless, airless—it will change. It will

not be broken; it will become unbreakable, impenetrable, irredeemable. . . . The only place outside Heaven where you can be perfectly safe from all the dangers . . . of love is Hell.[3]

# FAILURES

ANOTHER STUMBLING block involves the fear of failure. Reduce this book down to its most defining tension, and you'll find a tug-of-war between faith and the fear of failure. Unfortunately, the faithful mortal can never be completely fearless. But fear comes in degrees, and too many Christians view divine appointments with the fantastic imagination of a best-selling science fiction writer.

In chapter 7, I acknowledged the anxiety associated with Spirit-led interchanges and the need for approaching each one with a sense of relaxed anticipation. This deserves another pass because relaxed anticipation puts fear's root cause—failure—into a proper, faith-based perspective.

What is failure, after all? In every sporting contest one team fails to win. You could call that failure. But with proper coaching and the right attitude, the players get stronger and better equipped for the next encounter. Some Christians measure themselves with a stick God would never touch. It's the "either-or" stick—either this heaven-sent person trusts in Christ or does not. Next case.

But that mentality invites defeat before anyone shows up! It devalues the process just underway or already long since in play in the people you meet. So I'm fond of saying, "Where this goes, I don't know." Over the years, that seemingly nonchalant attitude has kept me available as Christ's mouthpiece and hands as well as protected me from needless migraines, ulcers, and premature gray hairs.

# THE TWO ANNAS

ONE OF my most vivid relaxed-anticipation stories took place during the summer of 1996 in Kiev, Ukraine, where I was conducting Your Home a Lighthouse seminars. My host, Victor Branitski, turned out to be my translator and a fast friend as well.

After a long day of ministry and speaking, he suggested making an impromptu ice cream run. That sounded mouthwatering. But before we caught a subway from our hotel for the ice cream parlor in downtown Kiev, I stuffed four Living Translation New Testaments in my barn jacket as an afterthought. I have never done that before or since, so the Holy Spirit must have moved me to grab those four copies.

Not surprisingly, we found the parlor packed with folks angling for sundaes, shakes, and malts. I couldn't help but notice that one table remained curiously empty amid the congestion. The Mafia reserved it with an iron fist. If a glossy black BMW or Mercedes pulled up, this jammed group knew to part like the Red Sea so those bad boys would have a place to sit. The corruption rankled me, but I bowed to the unwritten rule and meandered outside to find a table while Victor stood in the long line.

When I had stepped just a few paces from the parlor's front door onto the table-lined sidewalk, two well-dressed Ukrainian women in their early thirties invited me in perfect English to join them. As we chatted under the tilted red umbrella, Anna told me she was an environmental engineer and that her friend, who happened to also be named Anna, taught at a local college. Both wondered about my visit to their struggling country.

The question rang in my ears like the joyous sound of pealing church bells on Easter morning. Questions about my seminar work always do, because God uses them to pull the curtains up on one divine appointment after another.

After explaining the reason for my visit, my conversation with the Annas soon branched out. Using a slightly wrinkled paper napkin and ballpoint pen, I sketched the bridge Christ makes between God and us. Moments later, with the Annas' permission, I was leading a Lighthouse Bible study just feet away from the table reserved for the Mafia. Both women opened the Bibles I brought to page 120 where we thumbed to John 3:16 together. I pointed out that the Bible studies I promote hinge on this verse: "For God so loved the world that he gave his one and only Son, that whoever believes in him shall not perish but have eternal life."

Victor looked faintly confused when he reached our table with a dripping double-scooped dessert in each hand. His eyes wondered how I moved from taking a seat to leading a Lighthouse Bible study in downtown Kiev. But I temporarily ignored my friend's disorientation to put him on the spot. Could Victor tell us how God had changed his life? With no hesitation, he shared his compelling testimony in less than five minutes.

Here's the bottom line. The two Annas were not ready to receive Christ, but they each accepted a Bible, and we said good-bye with hopeful hearts. I can still see them—one in a bright red dress and the other in a business suit—each walking with a New Testament under her arm. Five years later, I still pray for them. My first granddaughter's name is Anna, which makes a good reminder. Did they ever read the Word or find Christ as Ukraine's post-communist state slowly recovered from its seventy-year anti-god chapter?

Regardless, a straight reading of this story shows a shut-down—the kind of "thanks-but-no-thanks" failure most fear. But that sells short the powerful potential of sown seeds. So again, I encourage you to view all exchanges as open-ended. In this broader context, the stumbling block of failure looks more like a stepping-stone to faith. Who knows? I may meet one Anna or two on those golden streets one day.

## BLESSED TO BLESS

IN MY years of working with Research & Development at DuPont, at least one hundred experiments failed for every success. I guess that experience helps me recognize that not all witnessing opportunities bring someone into the kingdom. Just as failures in R & D experiments brought us one step closer to a discovery, witnessing always brings that person closer to an ultimate decision.

In divine appointments as in science, forgiveness fits into the discovery process. You can expect to fumble, get tongue-tied, and balk when opportunities appear. What to say? What to do? Take a deep breath. The Holy Spirit frequently performs mighty works in the midst of human bumblings. He's been conditioned from age to age, after all. And remember that the most uptight Christian possesses something the secularist lacks—a sense of blessing. Sadly, however, not all believers regard this blessing highly enough to convincingly share it with others.

"I think it was Leighton Ford who told about a prostitute approaching a missionary," writes Stephen Brown in *No More Mr. Nice Guy!* "The missionary asked her price, and she told him. The missionary then said, 'Dear, that is not even close to enough. You are worth much more than that.' And then he told her about Christ."[4]

Prostitutes aren't the only ones who underestimate their value. Catholic priest Henri Nouwen also struggled to internalize his belovedness to God. This insecurity gnawed at him for years. In *Life of the Beloved,* he writes about those secular voices that too often sounded louder and more familiar than the sacred, still, small one. They pleaded, "Prove that you are worth something; do something relevant, spectacular or powerful, and then you will earn the love you so desire."[5]

On the other hand, if you embrace the richness of your blessing and mix that with 24/7 availability—look out! You may have to quit your day job because God's going to keep you busy. These winsome elements recently merged in one of the men I meet with on Fridays at the "barn" church. As a result, he slowly but surely became bolder for Christ.

## An Open Bible

RON LANZA started small. For instance, he read his Bible in public and just began waiting and watching for anything resembling a heaven-sent possibility. Gary Earl—the character who in chapter 6 discovered his wife's shockingly deep discontent—dashed into Dunkin' Donuts one day for a quick cup of coffee. When he spotted Ron reading the Word, he stopped in his tracks.

"You must be a Christian!" Gary exclaimed with a broad smile. After the two chatted a minute or two, Gary invited Ron to our Friday men's meeting. That's where I met him. All along, Ron figured he'd spot a divine appointment and then pray for the courage to step forward.

Surprisingly, the opportunity occurred when he noticed at the very same donut shop a 350-pound, leather-clad guy with dagger earrings, tattoos, and long hair. At first, Ron figured this couldn't possibly be someone God wanted him to talk to. However, after several mornings of brief eye contact, Ron bluntly asked, "Do you really believe that stuff?" referring to the man's dagger earrings.

That bold remark resulted in many conversations and a friendship. Ron eventually learned that Harry believed in good and evil, that he'd suffered child abuse growing up in Hartford foster homes, that he'd done jail time for assault, and that he currently worked as a cook at a biker bar.

Ron updates the men's group weekly, and we pray that one day he will lead Harry to Christ. He sees glimmers of faith in Harry, but no commitment thus far. Despite the gray zone, Ron continues mentoring the man and hoping that his blessing of faith will eventually bounce from him to Harry and on from there. Can you imagine how God can use the likes of Harry? They now go to local AA baseball games together, often taking Harry's daughter and some of his friends.

## "ZERO-DEPTH" CONTACT

RON DIDN'T accept Christ until middle age, and his encounter with Harry has been one of his most challenging opportunities to share his faith. Seeing Vietnam combat as a young man proved grisly and terrifying, but this divine appointment hit an 8.4 on the fear Richter scale compared to the 7.4 fear he felt in the rice paddies.

Nevertheless, he forged ahead by starting small, which leads to this reminder: To minister with maximum impact, a solid stepping-stone to divine appointments typically involves appreciating and ministering through "zero-depth" opportunities.

Picture your favorite beach. You and your Christian friends may have fun splashing around far out because you trust this great body of water to buoy you, and because you've learned something about navigating the waves. However, take five from your fun to scan the beach, and you'll notice the dominant nonswimmer population. Pre-seekers sunbathe—perfectly dry on their striped towels—while seekers scatter along the shoreline to occasionally dip in a toe.

Opportunities happen where the water and the sand meet—at zero depth. There, with some encouragement, seekers may wade up to their ankles and then their knees. Eventually, they may plunge past where they can touch on their tippy toes. So instead of always asserting the deep things of God, you might strike up a conversation about the weather or sports. Being a huge fan of the National Football League, tucking football talk into my traditional witnessing repertoire works well for me.

## EYE CONTACT

IN LUKE 5:27-28, the Bible says, "After this, Jesus went out and *saw* a tax collector by the name of Levi sitting at his tax booth" (emphasis added). We know from the first part of this story that Jesus saw; He had "eye contact." Then look what happens: "'Follow me,' Jesus said to him, and Levi got up, left everything and followed him."

I often say, "It's time for eye contact." That was certainly the starting point for Ron with Harry and Betty with Bryan Marcoux. Hence, in addition to casual conversation, consider upping your face time with unbelievers through friendship and service. Look for spiritual opportunities later. For instance, one neighbor near our Maine summer cottage remained anonymous to me for a couple of years. He would cruise past our driveway hunkered down in his fifteen-year-old blue Nissan, and he never ventured much past his backyard.

One dappled August afternoon last summer, I strolled over with a jar of Betty's homemade blueberry-raspberry jam and offered to weed-whack the bushy grass growing around his trees whenever I tended to our lawn. I've yet to experience a divine appointment with my neighbor, but I know I need to meet him before I will ever reach him with the claims of Christ.

These days, he drives by with his window rolled down and shouts a friendly, "Hello, Bob!" in passing. He surprised me last fall by stopping in to say, "Boy, you and your wife have done wonders with this place!" Only God knows where my relationship with him will go.

I got more eye contact with my neighbor by encouraging him to come out of his shell, but I know what it's like to be in one too. As a teenager, I remember feeling like an emotional hermit in the midst of a hopping church youth-group party. I had just started to notice the difference it made when a girl would sit by me rather than a boy. So when this gorgeous black-haired teenager with bright red lips, bobby socks, and a cardigan took a seat next to me on that scratchy mohair couch, the veins on my neck pushed out.

Before she noticed me, I felt extremely uncomfortable. Besides being the youngest kid at this party—I was a ninth grader and the other kids were juniors and seniors—I was puny for my age and painfully shy. But I've always been resourceful, so I had stashed a handful of hard candies in my pocket before I left home. If anyone started asking questions about my place at that party, I planned to distract them with a butterscotch or cinnamon disk.

Though we discussed nothing spiritual, I call that first couch talk with Betty a defining moment. For the first time, I thought Christians were approachable and *cool*. Because she was a couple of years older than me, I figured nothing romantic would ever come of us meeting. But there were other girls my age there, so I started attending Broadway Baptist Church in Parkersburg, West

Virginia. I got involved in the youth group and—several divine appointments later—I accepted Christ. And a few years later, during my junior year in college, Betty and I were married.

# MINISTRY KEYS

IN OUR spiritual journey and field experience, Betty and I have found again and again seven keys to effective ministry to those who don't know Jesus. They really summarize the major concepts of this book and assure us that God will put us in His place for divine appointments where we will see people come to faith in Christ and grow in their relationship with Him.

1. *Be part of God's family.* Unless a person has put his faith in Jesus Christ as Savior, he is not part of God's family. All who receive Christ are called the children of God (John 1:12). Being part of God's family is the home base for plainclothes ministry.

2. *Offer reckless abandonment to Christ.* This means that you are willing to give God everything—possessions, bank account, home, future, career, sex life—and to put Jesus on the throne of your life. Be ever willing to go *where* He leads *when* He leads. This total commitment seems like a sacrifice, but you may be surprised by the joy that comes from this kind of faith. I have yet to meet a totally committed Christian who felt miserable.

3. *Understand and apply the ministry of the Holy Spirit.* During the first eighteen years of my Christian life, the motives and purpose of the Holy Spirit completely confused me. However, Bill Bright's book, *The Christian and the Holy Spirit,* helped me more clearly understand the definition of His role. It changed my life. Now, instead of doing my own

thing, I let Him do His thing through me. Nowhere is this more critical than during divine appointments.

4. *Decide to go to where lost people live, work, and play.* Initially, Betty and I didn't know where to minister. Luke 4:18 clarifies the mission field by calling believers to go to the blind (spiritually), the brokenhearted, the captive, and the bruised wherever they may be.

5. *Get equipped.* Betty and I attended seminar after seminar to learn how to walk in the power of the Holy Spirit and to boldly share our faith. Besides the teaching we received at church, we also grew from material presented by parachurch groups like The Navigators and Campus Crusade for Christ.

6. *Identify your best platforms.* Early on, Betty and I decided to make our home and the workplace our two primary platforms, but your options are endless.

7. *Develop your team.* We recruited our first team when we lived in Wilmington, Delaware, during my years at DuPont. The circle included Larry and Sandy Vaughn and Les and Janet Berge. We started the Lighthouse Bible study movement together. Today, spin-off teams exist from Seattle to Southern California and from Canada to Florida. Jesus modeled teamwork because joint efforts encourage spiritual fruit.

## COINCIDENCE OR CALLING?

THESE STEPS will bring you closer to divine appointments. But, ultimately, your openness to recognizing and participating in divine appointments comes down to perspective. Do you view each one as a coincidence or a calling?

At a recent 8 A.M. Sunday service, my pastor, Dr. Jay Abramson, addressed this question of being called by God to fulfill His specific plans. To illustrate, he shared an inspiring anecdote from a movie:

> The movie *Simon Birch* that came out a few years ago told the story of a 12-year-old boy who suffered from a physical disability that prevented him from growing. At birth, he wasn't expected to live more than 24 hours, but he surprised everyone when he lived to be an adolescent.
>
> Though his miniature size disappointed his parents and made him the target of pranks and jokes from other kids, Simon embraced his condition and came to believe that God had put him on Earth for a special reason.
>
> One day, Simon went to speak with his pastor about this. He asked him, "Does God have a plan for us?"
>
> The minister replied, "I'd like to think so."
>
> Simon enthusiastically said, "Me, too. I think God made me the way I am for a reason."
>
> The minister stammered, "I'm glad that, um, that your faith, uh, helps you deal with your, um, you know, your condition."
>
> But Simon tells him, "That's not what I mean. I think I'm God's instrument. He's going to use me to carry out His plan."
>
> To which the minister says bluntly, "It's wonderful to have faith, son, but let's not overdo it."
>
> A short time later in the movie, Simon and his classmates are riding on a school bus over icy winter roads. The driver veers to avoid a deer, and the bus plunges into a lake. Everyone in the front of the bus escapes, but Simon and a handful of students in the back are trapped as the bus begins to sink. Simon takes charge. He opens a

window and directs everyone to climb out. Last of all, Simon goes out himself.

In the hospital later, Simon's friend Joe assures him that all the kids are all right. Simon says to his friend, "Did you see how the [kids] listened to me?"

Joe says, "Yeah."

With great satisfaction, Simon says, "That window was just my size."

Joe replies with a smile, "[Yeah], extra small."

Even as a small fry, Simon believed God called him to something big and something specific. He recognized his importance in God's plan, that he counted in ways he could not yet fathom. He considered himself an instrument designed for God's unique purposes and ready to meet those ends. As you ponder the mystery of divine appointments and weigh coincidence against calling, can you say the same? Your answer makes a difference.

# KEEPING
## APPOINTMENTS

1. Are you involved in a small-group Bible study? If so, do you agree that its two primary objectives should be to enhance your relationship with God and to help you reach out to unbelievers? Why or why not?

2. Would you consider yourself to be in a mission field? If so, how would you describe it?

3. By faith, can you love those in your world?

4. Bob recognized his encounter with the two Annas in Kiev as a divine appointment. How would you recognize a divine appointment?

5. Do you think the seven keys to building an effective equipping ministry would work in your life? Why or why not?

6. After reading this book, are there decisions you have made or need to make? What are those decisions?

# HOW TO EXPLAIN THE GOSPEL

THE FOLLOWING IS A simple way to explain the gospel. Once you learn these four simple steps, you will always be prepared to tell others how God enables us to have a personal relationship with Him. All you'll need is a pen and paper.

If the possibility of knowing God personally is a new concept to you, these steps will help you establish your relationship to Him. If you already have the assurance of knowing God, the steps will help you share your faith with others.

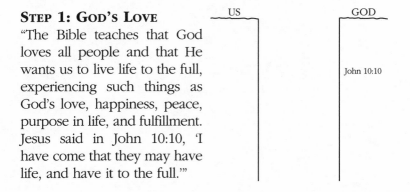

"I would like to draw an illustration that shows how God enables man to have a personal relationship with Him."

**STEP 1: GOD'S LOVE**

"The Bible teaches that God loves all people and that He wants us to live life to the full, experiencing such things as God's love, happiness, peace, purpose in life, and fulfillment. Jesus said in John 10:10, 'I have come that they may have life, and have it to the full.'"

US | GOD

John 10:10

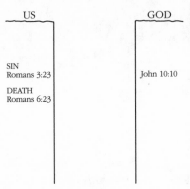

## STEP 2: MAN'S PROBLEM

"But given the choice of either keeping God's commandments (which would lead to a fulfilled life) or disobeying and centering our lives around ourselves, the human race chose to go its own way. This rebelliousness or even indifference to God is sin. Romans 3:23 says, 'All have sinned and fall short of the glory of God.' Sin leads to separation from God and eternal spiritual death. Romans 6:23 says, 'The wages of sin is death.' Humans cannot save themselves."

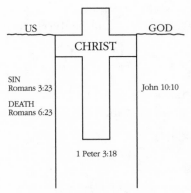

## STEP 3: GOD'S REMEDY

"But in spite of our sin, God still loves us and desires that we know Him personally. So He Himself paid the ransom for our lives. He sent His Son Jesus Christ to take upon Himself the penalty of our sin, so that we could be forgiven.

"And because Christ is both fully man and fully God—sinless in Himself and yet bearing our sin—He is the perfect bridge to save us and to restore us to a personal relationship with God. 1 Peter 3:18 says, 'Christ died for sins once for all, the righteous for the unrighteous, to bring you to God.'"

## Step 4: Our Response

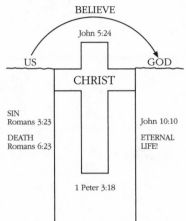

"But while Christ has made it possible for us to cross the bridge to intimate friendship with God, we are not automatically there. We need to take action that demonstrates our faith in what He has done. In prayer, we need to (1) acknowledge to God our sinfulness, (2) ask His forgiveness, which is available because of what Christ has done, and (3) ask Christ to take charge of our lives—to take first place in our thoughts and actions. Jesus says in John 5:24, 'Whoever hears my word and believes him who sent me has eternal life and will not be condemned; he has crossed over from death to life.'"

If the person you are sharing this diagram with indicates his or her readiness to receive Christ as Savior and Lord, suggest that the two of you pray together a prayer for salvation. Here is an example of such a prayer:

> Dear Lord, I acknowledge that I am a sinner and that I need Your forgiveness. I believe You love me and showed Your love by sending Your Son Jesus Christ to die for my sins. I trust in this alone to put me in a right relationship with You. I ask You to take over my life and live within me forever. Thank you.

# NOTES

CHAPTER 2: 24/7 AVAILABILITY
1. Oswald Chambers, *My Utmost for His Highest* (Uhrichsville, OH: Barbour Publishing, orig. ed. 1935).
2. Quoted in David McCasland, *Abandoned to God* (Uhrichsville, OH: Barbour Publishing, 1993), p. 156.
3. Bill Bright, *The Christian and the Holy Spirit* (Orlando, FL: NewLife Publications, 1994), pp. 29-30.

CHAPTER 4: GETTING EQUIPPED
1. Tommy Tenney, *The God Chasers* (Shippensburg, PA: Destiny Image Publishers, 1998), p. 114.
2. Charles Colson, *Against the Night* (Ann Arbor, MI: Vine Books, 1989), n.p.
3. Bill Bright, *The Christian and the Holy Spirit* (Orlando, FL: NewLife Publications, 1994), pp. 13-14.
4. Bill Bright, *The Holy Spirit: The Key to Supernatural Living* (Orlando, FL: NewLife Publications, 2000), p. 73.
5. Howard G. and William Hendricks, *As Iron Sharpens Iron* (Chicago: Moody, 1999), p. 183.

CHAPTER 5: TEAM BUILDING
1. Joseph C. Aldrich, *Discipleship Journal,* no. 54, p. 16.
2. *Discipleship Journal,* November–December 1989, p. 16.
3. C. S. Lewis, *The Weight of Glory* (Grand Rapids, MI: Eerdmans, 1949), p. 15.

CHAPTER 6: PLATFORMS FOR MINISTRY
1. Joseph C. Aldrich, *Discipleship Journal,* no. 54, p. 15.

CHAPTER 7: RELAXED ANTICIPATION
1. Charles R. Swindoll, *The Grace Awakening* (Dallas: Word, 1990), pp. 155-156.
2. Brennan Manning, *The Ragamuffin Gospel* (Sisters, OR: Multnomah, 1990, 2000), p. 101.
3. Manning, pp. 115-116.
4. Manning, p. 45.
5. Linda Dillow, *Calm My Anxious Heart* (Colorado Springs: NavPress, 1998), pp. 152-153.

CHAPTER 8: VEINS OF SPIRITUAL GOLD
1. Joseph C. Aldrich, *Gentle Persuasion* (Sisters, OR: Multnomah, 1988), p. 136.
2. Stephen Brown, *No More Mr. Nice Guy!* (Nashville: Nelson, 1986), p. 57.
3. Brown, p. 69.

CHAPTER 9: SIDE BY SIDE
1. Tim Hansel, *Holy Sweat* (Dallas: Word, 1987), pp. 26-27.
2. Lucinda Vardey, compiler, *Mother Teresa: Meditations from a Simple Path* (New York: Ballantine Books, 1996), p. 86.
3. Hansel, p. 55.
4. From *For Achievers Only,* June 1998, pp. 8-9.

CHAPTER 10: STUMBLING BLOCKS AND STEPPING-STONES
1. Tim Hansel, *Holy Sweat* (Dallas: Word, 1987), p. 161.
2. Joseph C. Aldrich, *Gentle Persuasion* (Sisters, OR: Multnomah, 1988), p. 8.
3. C. S. Lewis, *The Four Loves* (New York: Harcourt, Brace & World, 1960), p. 169.
4. Stephen Brown, *No More Mr. Nice Guy!* (Nashville: Nelson, 1986), p. 146.
5. Henri J. M. Nouwen, *Life of the Beloved* (New York: Crossroad Publishing Co., 1992), p. 29.

# AUTHORS

BOB JACKS is a businessman who began to reach out to nonChristians through home Bible studies around 1965. Through that ministry, he and his wife, Betty, wrote the NavPress book *Your Home a Lighthouse*, which is now published in four languages. Bob has had an ongoing ministry relationship with The Navigators for over fifteen years. He and Betty do seminars and speak at conferences, mostly related to living the victorious Christian life and how to reach out to a broken world.

∽    ∽    ∽

MATTHEW R. JACKS graduated from Philadephia College of Art and majored in sculpture and painting. He now lives in Lancaster, Pennsylvania, and owns his own company, which specializes in the reproduction of early American painted furniture and Civil War era children's clothing. Matthew hopes the message of this book will encourage churches to focus on people right in their own community who don't know Christ in a personal way.

∽    ∽    ∽

PAM MELLSKOG launched her freelance writing business in 1991 by creating radio jingles that aired over a five-state network in the upper Midwest. Pam coauthored a book entitled *A Patchwork Heart* (NavPress), and has written for Christian magazines such as *Children's Ministry, Christian Parenting Today*, and *Prism*. She resides in Boulder, Colorado.

# TELL US YOUR DIVINE APPOINTMENT STORIES!

YOU'VE JUST READ ABOUT the wonderful yet ordinary ways God is using the authors and their friends to impact lives through divine appointments.

Perhaps God has led you to divine appointments, or maybe you were the recipient of a divine appointment that changed your life. Or maybe the message of this book has changed your life. If so, please share your story by writing us at

Divine Appointments
c/o NavPress
P.O. Box 35001
Colorado Springs, CO 80935

# BEING A CHRISTIAN IS MORE THAN JUST COMING TO CHRIST.

## Intentional Disciplemaking

What does it take to make disciples in the local church? It takes an understanding of biblical discipleship, the right environment, and an intentional plan. Here is that guide.
(Ron Bennett)

## Design for Discipleship Series Bible Studies

This best-selling Bible study series features step-by-step lessons, from laying a foundation in Christ to ensuring unfailing hope.
(The Navigators)

## The Discipline of Grace

If you've ever struggled with the difference between your role and God's role in your growth as a Christian, this book will comfort and challenge you as you learn to rest in Christ while vigorously pursuing a life of holiness.
(Jerry Bridges)

## Spiritual Disciplines for the Christian Life

Drawn from the church's rich heritage, this book will guide you through disciplines— meditation, fasting, journaling, and stewardship—that can deepen your walk with God.
(Donald S. Whitney)

To get your copies, visit your local bookstore, call 1-800-366-7788, or log on to www.navpress.com. Ask for a FREE catalog of NavPress products. Offer #BPA.

NAVPRESS

BRINGING TRUTH TO LIFE
www.navpress.com